Resource Guide

A COMPREHENSIVE LISTING OF MEDIA FOR FURTHER STUDY

Compiled by
Dr. William L. Shulman

President, Association of Holocaust Organizations
Director, Holocaust Resource Center & Archives, New York

A B L A C K B I R C H P R E S S B O O K

W O O D B R I D G E , C O N N E C T I C U T

Acknowledgments

Many people have given generously of their time and knowledge during the development of this series. We would like to thank the following people in particular: Genya Markon, and the staff at the United States Holocaust Memorial Museum Photo Archives—Leslie Swift, Sharon Muller, Alex Rossino, and Teresa Pollin—for their talented guidance; and Dr. Michael Berenbaum, currently President and CEO of the Survivors of the Shoah Visual History Foundation and formerly Director of the Research Institute at the U.S. Holocaust Memorial Museum for his valuable editorial input and support of our efforts.

Dr. William L. Shulman, President of the Association of Holocaust Organizations and the Director of the Holocaust Resource Center & Archives at Queensborough Community College, merits special mention. As the series academic editor—as well as the compiler of Books 7 and 8—Dr. Shulman's guidance, insight, and dedication went far beyond the call of duty. His deep and thorough knowledge of the subject gave us all the critical perspective we needed to make this series a reality.

Published by Blackbirch Press, Inc.
260 Amity Road
Woodbridge, CT 06525

web site: http://www.blackbirch.com
e-mail: staff@blackbirch.com

©1998 Blackbirch Press, Inc.
First Edition

Printed in the United States of America

10 9 8 7 6 5 4 3 2 1

Cover: From left to right: A detail from the Arch of Titus in Rome, Italy, that shows the Romans carrying off the spoils of Jerusalem after 70 C.E. (Scala/Art Resource, NY); Austrian workers welcome the arrival of German troops in March 1938. Their sign reads "Sieg Heil to the Führer" (National Archives, Courtesy USHMM Photo Archives); Hitler visits Paris soon after his successful invasion of France in June 1940 (AP/Wide World Photos); captured Jews are marched to a deportation site during the Warsaw ghetto uprising in April 1943 (National Archives, courtesy USHMM Photo Archives); children peer out from behind the barbed wire at Auschwitz (State Archives of the Russian Federation, courtesy of USHMM Photo Archives); an American soldier offers cigarettes to eager prisoners at Allach—a sub-camp of Dachau—after liberation (National Archives, courtesy USHMM Photo Archives).

Library of Congress Cataloging-in-Publication Data

Shulman, William L.
    Resource Guide: a comprehensive listing of media for further study / compiled by William L. Shulman.
—1st ed.
        p.   cm. — (Holocaust)
    Includes index.
    Summary: Annotated lists of books and other materials, including videos and CD-ROMs, that support study of the Holocaust.
    ISBN 1-56711-208-0 (lib. bdg. : alk. paper)
    1. Holocaust, Jewish (1939–1945)—Juvenile literature—Bibliography. 2. Holocaust, Jewish (1939–1945)—Video catalogs. 3. Holocaust, Jewish (1939–1945)—CD-ROM catalogs. 4. Holocaust, Jewish (1939–1945)—Museums—Directories. [1. Holocaust, Jewish (1939–1945)—Bibliography.]
I. Title. II. Series: Holocaust (Woodbridge, Conn.)
Z6374.H6S46   1998   D804.34
016.94053'18—dc21
                                        97-19132
                                            CIP
                                            AC

CONTENTS

Web Sites and CD-ROMs

Museums and Resource Centers

Author Index

Subject Index

Introduction

During the last three decades, there has been an enormous increase in the amount of material available for the study of the Holocaust. Part of this is due to the opening of archives around the world, enabling scholars to do the research that is necessary to analyze and describe the events. Part of it is due to the willingness—indeed, the commitment of the survivors to record their memories of their experiences.

A major factor in the demand for this information has been the tremendous increase in Holocaust education, as evidenced by the opening of Holocaust museums and resource and education centers throughout the United States, Europe, and Israel; and the the teaching of the Holocaust, particularly in the United States, Israel, and Germany. All of these efforts are reinforced by the almost daily reports in the media about the impact of the Holocaust, both on nations and individuals.

This volume offers a guide to the resources available, at this point in time, for the study of the Holocaust. It incorporates standard works on the subject as well as some of the latest books and multimedia materials. Wherever possible, specifications and information for easy access are provided. Many libraries and Holocaust resource centers can help locate or can provide the materials listed.

Reading Levels

Determining the reading and viewing levels for the materials listed in this volume has been a somewhat arbitrary task, since motivation and interest will often determine a person's ability to understand the material. The following codes, however, will serve as general guidelines:

J = grades 7–8
H = grades 9–12
C = college and above

Bibliography

In the past decade, an enormous amount of literature has been published about the Holocaust. Hardly a month goes by without a new memoir, historical analysis, or story appearing in print. The following selection of books represents only a small percentage of the material that is currently available in print.

Key
J = grades 7–8 **H** = grades 9–12 **C** = college and above

General Reference Works

Michael Berenbaum, editor. *Witness to the Holocaust.* New York: HarperCollins, 1997.

An illustrated documentary history of the Holocaust that should be part of every library collection. It traces the history through survivor testimonies, letters, government documents, newspaper reports, and diary accounts. A chronology is included. **JHC**

Abraham J. Edelheit and Hershel Edelheit. *History of the Holocaust: A Handbook and Dictionary.* Boulder, CO: Westview Press, 1994.

This two-part volume combines an accessible overview of contemporary Jewish history with a dictionary of Holocaust terms. Its graphs and charts are of particular value for research. **JHC**

Hershel Edelheit and Abraham J. Edelheit. *A World in Turmoil: An Integrated Chronology of the Holocaust and World War II.* Westport, CT: Greenwood Press, 1991.

Hitler reviews troops, Nuremberg, 1938.

This chronology lists every significant event by date from 1933 through 1948. It includes name, place, and subject indexes. **JHC**

Martin Gilbert. *Macmillan Atlas of the Holocaust.* New York: Macmillan, 1982.

An excellent reference tool. It contains more than 300 maps and many photographs that trace the different phases of the Holocaust, from the antisemitic violence of prewar Germany to liberation. It also covers the victimization of non-Jewish civilians. **JHC**

Israel Gutman, editor. *Encyclopedia of the Holocaust.* Four volumes. New York: Macmillan, 1990.

This is an essential reference work for all students of the Holocaust. It has substantive articles on all the major subjects and individuals involved. **JHC**

Michael Marrus, editor. *The Nazi Holocaust: Articles on the Destruction of European Jews.* Westport, CT: Meckler Corporation, 1989.

The most comprehensive collection of articles on the subject to the date of publication. The series deals with such topics as writing on the Holocaust, the origins of the Holocaust, the "Final Solution," Jewish resistance, and the bystanders. **HC**

Geoffrey Wigoder, editor. *The Holocaust: A Grolier Student Library.* Four volumes. Danbury, CT: Grolier Educational, 1997.

This four-volume dictionary has extensive entries for each item. It includes photographs, maps, and illustrations. **JHC**

David S. Wyman, editor. *The World Reacts to the Holocaust.* Baltimore, MD: Johns Hopkins University Press, 1996.

A major scholarly reference work that traces the arguments and controversies involved in the efforts to come to terms with the Holocaust. It covers 22 countries and the United Nations. **C**

European Jewry Before the Holocaust

H. I. Bach. *The German Jew: A Synthesis of Judaism and Western Civilization 1730–1930.* New York: Litman Library, Oxford University Press, 1984.

This work begins with a brief background of German Jewish history in the Middle Ages and then traces Jewish cultural life in the eighteenth century. The bulk of the book is a description of the contributions made by Jews to nineteenth- and early twentieth-century German culture. **HC**

Hugh Coleman. *The Jews of Czechoslovakia.* Three volumes. Philadelphia: The Jewish Publication Society, 1986.

This collection of essays provides a comprehensive analysis of Jewish participation in Czech life between the two world wars. **HC**

Lucjan Dobroszycki and Barbara Kirschenblatt-Gimblett. *Image Before My Eyes: A Photographic History of Jewish Life in Poland.* New York: Schocken Books, 1977.

An album of some 300 photographs from the YIVO (Institute for Jewish Research) collection depicting Jewish life. **JHC**

Harriet Pass Freidenreich. *The Jews of Yugoslavia: A Quest for Community.* Philadelphia: The Jewish Publication Society, 1979.

The first part of this work traces the development of Jewish life and culture, focusing on the major cities of Zagreb, Belgrade, and Sarajevo. Part Two examines communal affairs on the local

---

and national levels. Part Three deals with political life and official government relations with the Jews. **HC**

Israel Gutman, Ezra Mendelsohn, Jehuda Reinharz, and Chone Shmeruk, editors. *The Jews of Poland Between Two World Wars.* Hanover, NH: University Press of New England, 1989.

Twenty-seven essays dealing with Jewish life in Poland. Among the topics dealt with are antisemitism, politics, economic and social spheres, patterns of religious life, literature and culture, and historiography. **HC**

Celia S. Heller. *On the Edge of Destruction: The Jews of Poland Between the Two World Wars.* New York: Schocken Books, 1979.

A historical and sociological discussion of the Jewish community in Poland in the 1920s and 1930s. The author also discusses cultural and political organizations. **HC**

Paula Hyman. *From Dreyfus to Vichy: The Remaking of French Jewry, 1906–1938.* New York: Columbia University Press, 1979.

An incisive study of the communal life of French Jewry in the generations before the Holocaust. It shows how the Jewish community in France was changed by the immigration of Eastern European Jews. **HC**

Jack Kuglemass and Jonathan Boyarin. *From a Ruined Garden: The Memorial Book of Polish Jewry.* New York: Schocken Books, 1983.

This collection of material from memorials written by Holocaust survivors describes the life of Jews before the war. **JHC**

Ezra Mendelsohn. *The Jews of East Central Europe Between the World Wars.* Bloomington, IN: Indiana University Press, 1983.

A major study of Jewish life in the region as well as the relationship between Jews and Gentiles. The author compares the "Western-type" Jewish communities of Czechoslovakia and

Hungary, where Jews were acculturated and assimilated, to the "Eastern-type" Jewries of Poland and Lithuania, where national movements were strong. **HC**

Catherine Noren. *The Camera of My Family.* New York: Alfred A. Knopf, 1976.

Photographs and mementos of five generations of a German Jewish family. Noren traces their history—using a series of wonderful photographs—from the nineteenth century, through the Holocaust, to their life in the United States. **JHC**

The Holocaust: A General Overview

David A. Altshuler. *Hitler's War Against the Jews—The Holocaust: A Young Reader's Version of the War Against the Jews 1933–1945 by Lucy Dawidowicz.* West Orange, NJ: Behrman House, 1978.

A shortened and simplified version of Dawidowicz's classic work The War Against the Jews 1933–1945. *An excellent one-volume introductory overview of the Holocaust.* **J**

Susan D. Bachrach. *Tell Them We Remember: The Story of the Holocaust.* Boston: Little, Brown, 1994.

This book tells the story of the Holocaust as presented in the United States Holocaust Memorial Museum. It is illustrated with artifacts and photographs and includes the stories of young people who suffered or were murdered during the Holocaust. **J**

Yehuda Bauer and Nili Keren. *A History of the Holocaust.* New York: Franklin Watts, 1982.

The most readable general history of the subject, this book examines the origins of antisemitism and Nazism as well as the history of Jewish–German relationships. **HC**

Michael Berenbaum. *The World Must Know: A History of the Holocaust as told in the United States Holocaust Memorial Museum.* Boston: Little, Brown, 1993.

The author presents the story of the Holocaust as told at the United States Holocaust Memorial Museum. An invaluable reference tool, the book is extensively illustrated with photographs from the museum's collection and provides many eyewitness accounts from its archives. **HC**

Lucy Dawidowicz, *The War Against the Jews 1933–1945.* New York: Bantam Books, 1986.

A sophisticated analysis of the subject, Dawidowicz argues that World War II was waged to implement Hitler's Final Solution. **C**

Martin Gilbert. *The Holocaust: A History of the Jews of Europe During the Second World War.* New York: Henry Holt, 1986.

Gilbert combines historical narrative with the personal testimony of survivors. He first provides a brief history of antisemitism prior to Hitler and then documents the Holocaust. **HC**

The Raboy family, Jews from the Ukraine, 1935.

Raoul Hilberg. *The Destruction of the European Jews.* Student text. New York: Holmes & Meier, 1985.

An abridged version of a classic three-volume edition that focuses on the methods used by the Nazis to destroy the Jews. **HC**

Nora Levin. *The Holocaust: The Nazi Destruction of European Jewry, 1933–1945.* New York: Schocken Books, 1973.

A standard work on the subject. The first part of the book is a chronological narrative; the second part describes those years country by country. **HC**

Seymour Rossell. *The Holocaust: The World and the Jews, 1933–1945*. West Orange, NJ: Behrman House, 1992.

A good introductory narrative for young students on the events of the Holocaust, from the rise of Nazism to the Eichmann trial. The book includes pictures, maps, charts, a chronology, and profiles of significant figures. **J**

Leni Yahil. *The Holocaust: The Fate of European Jewry, 1932–1945*. New York: Oxford University Press, 1991.

A chronological approach with an emphasis on the period 1941–1945. Because the book includes the latest research to the date of its publication, it is an excellent research tool. **HC**

Country/Cultural Studies

Samuel Abrahamson. *Norway's Response to the Holocaust: A Historical Perspective*. New York: Holocaust Library, 1991.

This study traces the history of the Norwegian Jewish community during this period. Among the topics covered are the rise of the Quisling Nazi Party, rescue efforts, and resistance. **HC**

Haim Avni. *Spain, the Jews, and Franco*. Philadelphia: The Jewish Publication Society, 1982.

Based on extensive interviews and documented materials, this work gives an account of the rescue of Jewish refugees from German-occupied countries by the Franco regime. **HC**

Eleanor H. Ayer. *Cities at War: Berlin*. New York: New Discovery, 1992.

A look behind the scenes in Berlin during the war years through the eyes, ears, and mouths of teenagers—both Jews and Gentiles. Illustrated with superb archival photographs. **JHC**

Randolph L. Braham. *The Politics of Genocide: The Holocaust in Hungary.* Two volumes. New York: Columbia University Press, 1981.

A definitive history tracing the destruction of Hungarian Jewry from the end of World War I to the Nuremberg Trials. Among the topics covered are the political history of the period, the ghettos, the Judenrate *(Jewish Councils), deportations, the treatment of foreign Jews, the attitudes and actions of Christian churches, and international reaction and intervention.* **HC**

Randolph L. Braham, editor. *The Tragedy of Romanian Jewry.* New York: Columbia University Press, 1994.

Nine essays by specialists dealing with a variety of topics, from prewar antisemitism through the Holocaust to antisemitism in the post-Communist era. **HC**

Frederick B. Chary. *The Bulgarian Jews and the Final Solution, 1940–1944.* Pittsburgh: University of Pittsburgh Press, 1972.

This study of the development of Bulgaria's policy toward the Jews during the Holocaust illustrates how citizens could try to thwart the implementation of Hitler's Final Solution. **HC**

Lucjan Dobroszycki and Jeffrey S. Gurock. *The Holocaust in the Soviet Union: Studies and Sources on the Destruction of the Jews in the Nazi Occupied Territories of the USSR, 1941–1945.* Armonk, NY: M. E. Sharpe, 1993.

The fullest available treatment of the deliberate massacre of the Jews in the Soviet Union. Among the topics dealt with are Soviet policies during the Holocaust and sources for the study of the Holocaust in the former Soviet Union. **HC**

Andrew Ezergailis. *The Holocaust in Latvia 1941–1944: The Missing Center.* Riga, Latvia: The Holocaust Institute of Latvia, 1996.

The first comprehensive study of the Holocaust in Latvia, the author describes the people and the military and SS units, both German and Latvian, that participated in the murder of the Jews. **HC**

Michael R. Marrus and Robert O. Paxton. *Vichy France and the Jews.* New York: Basic Books, 1981.

Comparing German documents with French sources, this book conclusively demonstrates that the Vichy government initiated a wave of antisemitic laws independent of German pressure. It proves that Vichy France collaborated in the Final Solution. **HC**

Meir Michaelis. *Mussolini and the Jews: German–Italian Relations and the Jewish Question in Italy 1922–1945.* New York: Oxford University Press, 1978.

The first part of this book shows that Mussolini wanted to convince the Jews to become Fascists as part of his imperial policy. The second part shows the influence of the Axis alliance on Italian Fascist policy. **C**

Dina Porat. *The Blue and the Yellow Stars of David: The Zionist Leadership in Palestine and the Holocaust, 1939–1945.* Cambridge, MA: Harvard University Press, 1990.

This work describes how and when the Zionist leadership in Palestine fully understood that the Jews of Europe were facing annihilation. The book examines the rescue plans they developed and the resources allocated to these efforts. It examines what went wrong with the Zionists' plans and why, in the end, so little was done to help the Jews. **C**

Hannu Rautkallio. *Finland and the Holocaust.* New York: Holocaust Library, 1987.

This book contains a background history of the Jews of Finland as well as an account of their experience during the Holocaust and World War II. **HC**

Gertrude Schneider. *Exile and Destruction: The Fate of Austrian Jews, 1938–1945*. Westport, CT: Praeger, 1995.

This book provides a detailed account of how the Jews lived in Austria from 1938 to 1945 until they either fled or were deported. A list of all the Austrian concentration-camp survivors is included. **HC**

Victoria Sherrow. *Cities at War: Amsterdam*. New York: New Discovery, 1992.

A behind-the-scenes view of Amsterdam during the war years, through the eyes and in the words of teenagers—both Jews and Gentiles—who endured the German regime. **JHC**

Susan Zuccotti. *The Holocaust, The French and the Jews*. New York: Basic Books, 1993.

This book examines the response of the French people to the Holocaust. Drawing on memoirs, government documents, and the interviews of survivors, it describes the reactions of ordinary French people, both Jews and non-Jews, to those events. **HC**

Susan Zuccotti. *The Italians and the Holocaust: Persecution, Rescue and Survival*. New York: Basic Books, 1987; paperback edition, Lincoln, NE: University of Nebraska Press, 1996.

A well-written narrative that weaves together personal histories and historical analysis. Zuccotti raises fundamental questions about human behavior in times of crisis. **HC**

Germany, Hitler, and the Rise of Nazism

William S. Allen. *The Nazi Seizure of Power: The Experience of a Single German Town, 1922–1945*. New York: Franklin Watts, 1984.

A detailed, local study of Northeim, a town in central Germany, illustrating the impact of Nazism on a single community. **HC**

William Carr. *A History of Germany: 1815–1985*. Baltimore: Edward Arnold, 1987.

A readable general history. **HC**

Gordon A. Craig. *Germany: 1866–1945*. New York: Oxford University Press, 1978.

The author traces the history of modern Germany from the period of Otto von Bismarck to the end of World War II. He examines closely the people, parties, and pressure groups that influenced foreign and domestic policy. **HC**

John V. H. Dippel. *Bound Upon a Wheel of Fire: Why So Many German Jews Made the Tragic Decision to Remain in Nazi Germany*. New York: Basic Books, 1996.

The story of six prominent German Jews who, because of their love for their country, decided to remain in Germany. **HC**

Joachim C. Fest. *Hitler*. New York: Harcourt Brace Jovanovich, 1974.

A good biography of Hitler that examines the roots of his beliefs and traces his rise to and fall from power. It contains little information about the Holocaust. **C**

Saul Friedlander. *Nazi Germany and the Jews: Volume 1, The Years of Persecution, 1933–1939*. New York: HarperCollins, 1997.

Making extensive use of new documentation, Friedlander shows how one of the world's most culturally and industrially advanced nations embarked on a path that led toward the extermination of Jews. It is the most important work on the subject to date. **HC**

Sarah Gordon. *Hitler, Germans and the Jewish Question*. Princeton, NJ: Princeton University Press, 1984.

This book discusses a number of related questions about the role of antisemitism in the rise of Nazism. **HC**

Anton Kaes, Martin Jay, and Edward Dimendberg, editors. *The Weimar Republic Sourcebook*. Berkeley, CA: University of California Press, 1994.

This is the most comprehensive single volume on the subject. It includes a variety of primary sources covering the years of the Weimar Republic. **HC**

Michael H. Kater. *The Nazi Party: A Social Profile of Members and Leaders, 1919–1945*. Cambridge, MA: Harvard University Press, 1983.

This book gives an excellent analysis of the personnel and structure of the Nazi movement. **HC**

Claudia Koonz. *Mothers in the Fatherland: Women, the Family and Nazi Politics*. New York: St. Martin's Press, 1988.

A history of the women's movement in Germany from the Weimar Republic to the Nazi period, emphasizing the role of women in Nazi Germany and the impact of Nazism on the family unit. It includes material on the influence of the Church in defining women's roles, on female members of the resistance, and on Jewish women. **C**

Albert Marrin. *Hitler: A Portrait of a Tyrant*. New York: Viking, 1987.

The most detailed study of Hitler and Nazism available for young people. **J**

Hans Mommsen. *The Rise and Fall of Weimar Democracy*. Chapel Hill, NC: University of North Carolina Press, 1996.

This is an English translation of the major work of one of Germany's preeminent historians. It is Mommsen's definitive analysis of the social, economic, and political developments in Germany between the end of World War I and Hitler's coming to power in 1933. **HC**

George Mosse. *Nazi Culture: A Documentary History*. New York: Schocken Books, 1981.

An anthology of source material with introductions to each section and selection, this work includes material taken from speeches, newspapers, diaries, and contemporary literature. **JHC**

Louis L. Snyder. *Hitler and Nazism*. New York: Bantam Books, 1967.

A biography of Hitler and a brief history of the main events of the Third Reich. **J**

John Weiss. *Ideology of Death: Why the Holocaust Happened in Germany*. Chicago: Ivan R. Dee, 1996.

A well-written narrative that traces the culture of racism and antisemitism among both the elite and ordinary people. Weiss describes how the Nazis appealed to a wide variety of groups in order to achieve political success. **HC**

Ghettos

Yitzhak Arad. *Ghetto in Flames: The Struggle and Destruction of the Jews in Vilna in the Holocaust*. New York: Holocaust Library, 1982.

A detailed study of the Jewish Lithuanian community in Vilnius (Vilna), covering such topics as the German military and civil administrations, the internal organization of and life in the ghetto, resistance, and liquidation. **HC**

Lucjan Dobroszycki, editor. *The Chronicle of the Lodz Ghetto 1941–1944*. New Haven, CT: Yale University Press, 1984.

This chronicle provides a detailed look at everyday life in the Lodz ghetto, a sealed community that was under enormous stress. The footnotes and the introduction provide analyses of the material and give a history of the ghetto. **C**

Yisrael Gutman. *The Jews of Warsaw, 1939–1943: Ghetto, Underground, Revolt.* Bloomington, IN: Indiana University Press, 1982.

The most authoritative work to date on the history of the Warsaw ghetto, from its creation by the Nazis to its liquidation. **C**

Raoul Hilberg, et al., editors. *The Warsaw Diary of Adam Czerniakow.* Lanham, MD: Madison Books, 1982.

This journal is one of the most important documents testifying to the agony of living in the Warsaw ghetto before the deportations. **HC**

Emanuel Ringelblum. *Notes from the Warsaw Ghetto: The Journal of Emanuel Ringelblum.* New York: Schocken Books, 1974.

Ringelblum was the official archivist of the Warsaw ghetto who documented events on a daily basis. An invaluable source. **HC**

Gertrude Schneider. *Journey into Terror: The Story of the Riga Ghetto.* New York: Ark House, 1979.

Based on Nazi documents, interviews with survivors, and her own diary, Schneider traces the history of and life in the major ghetto in Latvia. **HC**

Zvi Szner and Alexander Sened, editors. *With a Camera in the Ghetto.* New York: Schocken Books, 1987.

Mendel Grossman was a Jewish photographer who, under extremely difficult conditions, was able to depict on film life in the Lodz ghetto. This is a remarkable collection of pictures. **HC**

Isaiah Trunk. *Judenrat: The Jewish Councils in Eastern Europe Under Nazi Occupation.* New York: Stein & Day, 1977.

The most important study of the Jewish Councils and their relationship with the Jewish community and with the German authorities. The book deals with the conditions under which the Councils operated, the motivations of the members, and the results of their activities. **C**

Concentration and Extermination Camps

Paul Berben. *Dachau 1933–1945*. London: Comite International de Dachau, 1975.

A history of the Dachau camp based on historical records and survivor testimony. It covers all aspect of camp life from its creation to its liberation. **C**

Danuta Czech. *Auschwitz Chronicle 1939–1945*. New York: Henry Holt, 1990.

The only published portion of the records of Auschwitz throughout the period of its existence, this is an essential reference tool. **HC**

Terrence Des Pres. *The Survivor: An Anatomy of Life in the Death Camps*. New York: Oxford University Press, 1976.

One of the most important memoirs from the camps. The author studies survivors and attempts to determine the factors that enabled them to survive. **C**

Thousands of gold rings that had been taken from prisoners at Buchenwald.

Deborah Dwork and Robert Jan van Pelt. *Auschwitz: 1270 to the Present*. New York: W. W. Norton, 1996.

A beautifully written and illustrated history of the town of Auschwitz (called Oswiecim in Polish) and the camps of Auschwitz–Birkenau. It shows how an ordinary town became the most infamous killing center in history. **HC**

Konnilyn G. Feig. *Hitler's Death Camps: The Sanity of Madness*. New York: Holmes & Meier, 1981.

An excellent, well-documented account of each of the major concentration and death camps. **HC**

Yisrael Gutman and Michael Berenbaum, editors. *Anatomy of the Auschwitz Death Camp.* Bloomington, IN: Indiana University Press, 1994.

A collection of scholarly essays that covers all aspects of Auschwitz-Birkenau, such as the construction and operation of the camps, the perpetrators, and the victims. **C**

David A. Hackett, editor. *The Buchenwald Report.* Boulder, CO: Westview Press, 1995.

The first liberated camp in western Germany was Buchenwald, (April 11, 1945). This report, prepared by U.S. Army intelligence officers, describes in detail the camp's history, organization, functioning, and daily life. Eyewitness accounts are included. **C**

Eugen Kogen. *The Theory and Practice of Hell: The German Concentration Camps and the System Behind Them.* New York: Berkeley Publishing, 1982.

First printed in 1950, this graphic study of the concentration camps was used as a basis for the Nuremberg Trials. This work is appropriate only for adults. **C**

Primo Levi. *Survival in Auschwitz.* New York: Macmillan, 1987.

This is the memoir of an Italian Jew captured in 1943 and sent to Auschwitz–Birkenau. In it, he chronicles the daily activities in the camp and reflects upon his experiences. **HC**

Elie Wiesel. *Night.* New York: Bantam Books, 1982.

This compelling narrative describes Wiesel's own experience in Auschwitz. It is a book that all students of the Holocaust must read. **JHC**

Resistance

Resistance and rescue were often connected. Indeed, rescue was a form of resistance. This section is primarily concerned with armed resistance.

Israel Gutman. *Resistance: The Warsaw Ghetto Uprising*. Boston: Houghton Mifflin, 1994.

> *A study of the uprising in the Warsaw ghetto, this work contains excerpts from diaries, letters, and other documents from the period.* **HC**

Theodore S. Hamerow. *On the Road to the Wolf's Lair: German Resistance to Hitler*. Cambridge, MA: Harvard University Press, 1997.

> *An unsparing history of German resistance in high places. It raises important moral and historical questions.* **HC**

Shmuel Krakowski. *The War of the Doomed: Jewish Armed Resistance in Poland, 1942–1944*. New York: Holmes & Meier, 1984.

> *This book tells the story of Jewish armed resistance in the Polish forests, in Polish partisan and commando units, in the cities, and in prisoner-of-war and extermination camps.* **HC**

Vera Laska. *Women in the Resistance and in the Holocaust: The Voices of Eyewitnesses*. Westport, CT: Greenwood Publishing, 1983.

> *More than two dozen first-person accounts of women from different countries during the Holocaust. The book deals with their roles in resistance and their experiences in hiding and in the camps.* **C**

Anny Latour. *The Jewish Resistance in France (1940–1944)*. New York: Holocaust Library, 1981.

> *This book tells the story of Jews in occupied France who developed*

programs to protect Jewish children and provide Jewish adults with hiding places and safe passage out of the country. **HC**

Dov Levin. *Fighting Back: Lithuanian Jewry's Armed Resistance to the Nazis, 1941–1945.* New York: Holmes & Meier, 1985.

The first comprehensive account of Jewish resistance in Lithuania. Major topics discussed are Jewish soldiers in the Red Army, partisan warfare, and resistance in the ghettos and labor camps. **HC**

Vladka Meed. *On Both Sides of the Wall.* New York: Holocaust Library, 1979.

The story of one young woman who helped to smuggle weapons and ammunition into the Warsaw ghetto. **HC**

Inge Scholl. *The White Rose: Munich, 1942–1943.* Middletown, CT: Wesleyan University Press, 1983.

The story of the White Rose movement, the attempt by a group of young Christian Germans to protest the Nazi movement. The book includes original documents. **HC**

Bea Stadtler. *The Holocaust: A History of Courage and Resistance.* New York: Behrman House, 1973.

A history for young people that focuses on the topic of resistance. **J**

Yuri Suhl, editor. *They Fought Back: The Story of the Jewish Resistance in Nazi Europe.* New York: Schocken Books, 1975.

A collection of writings describing the wide range of resistance efforts by Jews during the Holocaust. **HC**

Marie Syrkin. *Blessed Is the Match: The Story of Jewish Resistance.* Philadelphia: The Jewish Publication Society, 1976.

First published in 1947, this work is a good introduction to the subject of Jewish resistance. **JHC**

Nechama Tec. *Defiance: The Bielski Partisans*. New York: Oxford University Press, 1993.

The story of a group of Jewish partisans who survived in the forests of White Russia (present-day Belarus). It was the largest armed rescue operation of Jews by Jews in World War II. **HC**

Yitzhak Zuckerman. *A Surplus of Memory: Chronicle of the Warsaw Ghetto Uprising*. Berkeley, CA: University of California Press, 1993.

The story of the uprising in the Warsaw ghetto by one of its leaders, "Antek." It tells of the daily struggle to survive under the terrible conditions in the ghetto. **HC**

Rescue

Gay Block and Malka Drucker. *Rescuers: Portraits of Moral Courage in the Holocaust*. New York: Holmes & Meier, 1992.

Interviews and color photographs of people from many countries who risked their lives to help Jews. The book includes an overview of the rescue efforts in each country covered. **HC**

Harold Flender. *Rescue in Denmark*. New York: Holocaust Library, 1963.

This book tells of the skill and daring of the Danes who hid the Jews of Denmark and later smuggled them to Sweden. **JHC**

Eva Fogelman. *Conscience and Courage: Rescuers of Jews During the Holocaust*. New York: Anchor Books, 1994.

Stories of individual Christians and their efforts to save Jews during the Holocaust. **HC**

Philip Friedman. *Their Brothers' Keepers: The Christian Heroes and Heroines Who Helped the Oppressed Escape the Nazi Terror*. New York: Crown Publishers, 1957.

A moving story of Christians from all walks of life who saved their fellow citizens during the Holocaust; a good overview of rescue activities. **JHC**

Miep Gies and Alison L. Gold. *Anne Frank Remembered: The Story of the Woman Who Helped to Hide the Frank Family.* New York: Simon & Schuster, 1988.

Miep Gies was among those who helped to hide the Frank family from the Nazis. This account is an important contribution to our understanding of that event. **HC**

Howard Greenfield. *The Hidden Children.* New York: Ticknor & Fields, 1993.

A collection of experiences, as told by the survivors, of Jewish children who were hidden during the Holocaust. **J**

Phillip Hallie. *Lest Innocent Blood Be Shed: The Story of the Village of Le Chambon and How Goodness Happened There.* New York: Harper & Row, 1979.

A remarkable and inspiring story of the villagers in southern France who, led by their clergy, saved Jews. **HC**

Peter Hellman. *Avenue of the Righteous.* New York: Atheneum, 1980.

A collection of stories about Christians who saved Jews. **JHC**

Lucien Lazare. *Rescue as Resistance: How Jewish Organizations Fought the Holocaust in France.* New York: Columbia University Press, 1996.

The story of how Jewish French resistance groups launched effective rescue and relief efforts. **C**

Eleanor Lester. *Wallenberg: The Man in the Iron Web.* Englewood Cliffs, NJ: Prentice Hall, 1982.

This carefully documented work traces Raoul Wallenberg's life until his disappearance during the war. **JHC**

Milton Meltzer. *Rescue: The Story of How Gentiles Saved Jews in the Holocaust.* New York: Harper & Row, 1988.

Dozens of stories about Righteous Gentiles trying to defy the Nazi plan to exterminate the Jews. **J**

Dalia Ofer. *Escaping the Holocaust: Illegal Immigration to the Land of Israel, 1939–1944.* New York: Oxford University Press, 1990.

An examination of various rescue and illegal immigration efforts organized by the Palestine Jewish community. **C**

Samuel Oliner and Kathleen Lee. *Who Shall Live: The Wilhelm Backner Story.* Chicago: Academy Chicago Publishers, 1996.

The biography of a Jew who saved more than 50 Jews and Gentiles from Nazi injustice. **JHC**

Alexander Ramati. *The Assisi Underground, The Priests Who Rescued Jews.* New York: Stein and Day, 1978.

The story of the priests of the Italian town of Assisi who risked their lives to save Jews. **JHC**

This portrait was taken at the confirmation ceremony for Janina Nebel, a Jewish girl who was hidden by Leokadia Nawrocka, a Gentile Pole.

Carol Rittner and Sondra Meyers, editors. *The Courage to Care: Rescuers of the Jews During the Holocaust.* New York: New York University Press, 1989.

Short essays about rescuers and those they rescued from various countries, with historical commentary. **HC**

Maxine B. Rosenberg. *Hiding to Survive: Stories of Jewish Children Rescued from the Holocaust.* New York: Clarion Books, 1994.

The stories of men and women from different countries who relate their experiences as "hidden children" and tell about their rescuers. **JH**

Eric Silver. *The Book of the Just: The Unsung Heroes Who Rescued Jews from Hitler*. New York: Grove Press, 1992.

This book tells the story of individuals who risked their lives to save Jews during the Holocaust. **HC**

Andre Stein, *Quiet Heroes: True Stories of the Rescue of Jews by Christians in Nazi-Occupied Holland*. New York: New York University Press, 1988.

Seven tales of rescue, told in the words of the rescuers. **JHC**

Nechama Tec. *Dry Tears: The Story of a Lost Childhood*. Westport, CT: Wildcat Publishers, 1982.

This autobiography of a "hidden child" gives insight into the complex issues of rescue and resistance. **HC**

Nechama Tec. *When Light Pierced the Darkness: Christian Rescue of Jews in Nazi-Occupied Poland*. New York: Oxford University Press, 1986.

Based on her own experiences and extensive research, Nechama Tec describes what it was like to be both a rescuer and one who was rescued during the Holocaust. **HC**

Leni Yahil. *The Rescue of Danish Jewry: Test of a Democracy*. Philadelphia: The Jewish Publication Society, 1969.

The most authoritative work on the rescue of Danish Jews. **HC**

Perpetrators, Bystanders, and Collaborators

Irving Abella and Harold Troper. *None Is Too Many: Canada and the Jews of Europe 1933–1948*. New York: Random House, 1983.

Canada had one of the worst—if not the worst—record of all possible refugee-receiving nations. This well-documented book explains why. **C**

Yitzhak Arad, Shmuel Krakowski, and Shmuel Spector, editors. *The Einsatzgruppen Reports*. New York: Holocaust Library, 1989.

These selected dispatches are from the Nazi death squads' campaign against the Jews between July 1941 and January 1943. They are primary evidence of the Nazis' murder of Jews. **C**

Christopher Browning. *Ordinary Men: Reserve Police Battalion 101 and the Final Solution in Poland*. New York: HarperCollins, 1992.

This powerful book tells the story of "ordinary men" who, through their own testimony, rationalize their participation in the Final Solution. It raises basic moral questions. **C**

Henry L. Feingold. *The Politics of Rescue: The Roosevelt Administration and the Holocaust 1938–1945*. New York: Holocaust Library, 1970.

A thorough, scholarly, and balanced analysis of American policy during the Holocaust. **HC**

Martin Gilbert. *Auschwitz and the Allies*. New York: Holt, Rinehart & Winston, 1981.

This book shows, on the basis of documentary evidence, how the Allies failed to act even when they had concrete information about the Holocaust. The book raises important moral questions. **HC**

Alfred A. Hasler. *The Lifeboat Is Full*. New York: Funk & Wagnells, 1969.

A documentary account of the responses of the Swiss people and the Swiss bureaucracy to the plight of Jews fleeing Nazi Germany. **HC**

Raoul Hilberg. *Perpetrators Victims Bystanders: The Jewish Catastrophe 1933–1945*. New York: HarperCollins, 1992.

This book provides an excellent introduction to who the perpetrators and bystanders were during the Holocaust. **HC**

Gordon Horowitz, *In the Shadow of Death: Living Outside the Gates of Mauthausen*. New York: The Free Press, 1990.

This book raises important questions about the complicity of bystanders. **C**

Michael H. Kater. *Doctors Under Hitler.* Chapel Hill, NC: University of North Carolina Press, 1989.

A history of medicine and of the medical profession in the Third Reich. It shows the devotion of some German doctors to Nazi ideology and the role they played in exterminating the Jews and other "undesirable" groups. **C**

Ernst Klee, et al., editors. *The Good Old Days: The Holocaust as Seen by Its Perpetrators and Bystanders.* New York: The Free Press, 1991.

This collection of material was taken from letters, diaries, reports, and other documents written by those who perpetrated and approved of the Holocaust. **C**

Michael R. Marrus and Robert O. Paxton. *Vichy France and the Jews.* New York: Basic Books, 1981.

A detailed and comprehensive account of the Vichy government's antisemitic policies and practices. It shows how, independent of German pressure, Vichy France unleashed its own attack on the Jews. **HC**

Richard L. Miller. *Nazi Justiz: Law of the Holocaust.* Westport, CT: Praeger, 1995.

This book documents the transformation of the German legal system into a criminal organization and shows how it shaped everyday life under the Nazis. It also explains how many Germans benefited from the Holocaust. **C**

John F. Morely. *Vatican Diplomacy and the Jews During the Holocaust 1939–1943*. New York: Ktav Publishing House, 1980.

This book investigates the Vatican's role during World War II and shows that it was well informed about the Nazis' Final Solution. **C**

David S. Wyman. *The Abandonment of the Jews: America and the Holocaust 1941–1945*. New York: Pantheon Books, 1984.

This book raises many questions about the United States' role during the Holocaust. It is a devastating condemnation of the government's policies. **C**

Other Victims of Nazi Persecution

Michael Berenbaum, editor. *A Mosaic of Victims: Non-Jews Persecuted and Murdered by the Nazis*. New York: New York University Press, 1990.

This collection of essays includes material on Romani (Gypsies), Serbs, Slavs, pacifists, and German and Austrian male homosexuals. **C**

Henry Friedlander. *The Origins of Nazi Genocide: From Euthanasia to the Final Solution*. Chapel Hill, NC: University of North Carolina Press, 1995.

This book examines how the Nazi program of secretly eliminating the mentally and physically disabled evolved into the systematic destruction of the Romani and Jews. **C**

Ina R. Friedman. *The Other Victims: First-Person Stories of Non-Jews Persecuted by the Nazis*. Boston: Houghton Mifflin, 1990.

Through a series of interviews, the author relates the suffering of Romani, Jehovah's Witnesses, the disabled, and other victims under Nazi rule. **J**

Hugh Gregory Gallagher. *By Trust Betrayed: Patients, Physicians, and the License to Kill in the Third Reich.* Arlington, VA: Vandemeer Press, 1995.

A compelling account of Nazi Germany's so-called euthanasia program, which enabled German physicians to kill the mentally and physically handicapped, whom the Nazis considered "unworthy of life." **C**

Richard Plant. *The Pink Triangle: The Nazi War Against Homosexuals.* New York: Henry Holt, 1986.

The author examines the reasons behind the Nazi persecution and incarceration of male homosexuals. **HC**

Liberation and Judgment

Robert H. Abzug. *Inside the Vicious Heart: Americans and the Liberation of Nazi Concentration Camps.* New York: Oxford University Press, 1985.

Abzug uses diaries, letters, photographs, and oral histories to analyze the reactions of the first witnesses to enter the liberated camps in Germany and Austria. **HC**

Robert E. Conot. *Justice at Nuremberg.* New York: Carroll & Graf, 1984.

A history of the Nuremberg Trials and their preparation. **HC**

Alan S. Rosenbaum. *Prosecuting Nazi War Criminals.* Boulder, CO: Westview Press, 1993.

Rosenbaum explains why we must continue to prosecute the perpetrators of the Holocaust. **C**

Otto Ohlendorf, former member of the *Einsatzgruppen*, is sentenced to death at the trial in Nuremberg, 1947.

Telford Taylor. *The Anatomy of the Nuremberg Trials: A Personal Memoir.* New York: Alfred A. Knopf, 1992.

A detailed account of the inner workings of the trials and the behavior of the defendants. **C**

Simon Wiesenthal. *The Sunflower: On the Possibilities and Limits of Forgiveness.* Revised edition. New York: Schocken Books, 1997.

This unusual account of an encounter between a survivor and a perpetrator raises basic moral questions about the limits and possibilities of forgiveness. **JHC**

Memoirs and Diaries

Inge Auerbacher. *I Am a Star: Child of the Holocaust.* New York: Prentice Hall, 1987.

As a child, Auerbacher was imprisoned in Theresienstadt concentration camp from 1942 to 1945. This book is an excellent and personalized introduction to the Holocaust. **J**

Charlotte Delbo. *None of Us Will Survive.* Boston: Beacon Press, 1968.

An eloquent and powerful memoir of Delbo's experiences at Auschwitz. **C**

Alexander Donat. *The Holocaust Kingdom.* New York: Holocaust Library, 1978.

The story of a Polish Jew whose experiences included time in the Warsaw ghetto, Majdanek, and Dachau. **C**

Olga Levy Drucker. *Kindertransport.* New York: Henry Holt, 1992.

One of many Jewish children evacuated from Germany to England in 1938–1939, the author relates her experiences in a simple and moving way. **J**

Toby Knobel Fluek. *Memories of My Life in a Polish Village 1930–1949.* New York: Alfred A. Knopf, 1990.

This is the story of a young Jewish girl growing up in a Polish farm village, from the peaceful early 1930s to the Holocaust. Illustrated with her own drawings. **J**

Anne Frank. *The Diary of a Young Girl.* The Definitive Edition. New York: Doubleday, 1995.

The eloquent memoir of an adolescent Jewish girl growing up during the Holocaust. One of the most widely read books of Holocaust literature. **JHC**

Luba Gurdus. *The Death Train.* New York: Holocaust Library, 1987.

The author writes about the time she and her family spent on or near trains in an unsuccessful attempt to avoid deportation to the camps. Illustrated with her original drawings. **HC**

Gizelle Hersh and Peggy Mann. *Gizelle, Save the Children.* New York: Everest House, 1980.

A remarkable story of survival and family cohesiveness in the face of destruction. **HC**

Etty Hillsum. *An Interrupted Life.* New York: Pocket Books, 1991.

Hillsum's diary notes from 1941 to 1942 and letters to family and friends from the Westerbork transit camp in German-occupied Holland are a remarkable testimony to the human spirit. **C**

Gerda Weissman Klein. *All But My Life.* New York: Hill and Wang, 1995.

A wonderful autobiography and testimony of the Holocaust. It is also a powerful love story. **HC**

Marie Rut Krizkova, Kurt Jiri Kotouc, and Zdenek Ornest. *We Are Children Just the Same: Vedem, the Secret Magazine by the Boys of Terezin*. Philadelphia: The Jewish Publication Society, 1995.

From 1942 to 1944, a group of 13- to 15-year-old Jewish boys secretly produced a weekly magazine in the Theresienstadt concentration camp. The material, saved by one of the boys who survived, is a poignant look at their struggle to survive. **JHC**

Isabella Leitner. *The Big Lie: A True Story*. New York: Scholastic, 1992.

An adaptation of Fragments of Isabella *for young people.* **J**

Isabella Leitner. *Fragments of Isabella: A Memoir of Auschwitz*. New York: Dell Publishing, 1983.

An eloquent account by a survivor of Auschwitz. **HC**

Primo Levi. *Survival in Auschwitz*. New York: Macmillan, 1987.

Levi, an Italian Jew, describes his life in Auschwitz–Birkenau. This is one of the most widely read and important memoirs of life in a camp. **HC**

Deportation from Westerbork transit camp, circa 1943.

Vladka Meed. *On Both Sides of the Wall*. New York: Holocaust Library, 1979.

Vladka Meed was not only an eyewitness to the Holocaust and the resistance efforts but was also an active participant in the battle for survival both inside and outside the Warsaw ghetto. **HC**

Johanna Reiss. *The Upstairs Room*. New York: HarperCollins, 1990.

The memoir of a Dutch Jewish girl who was hidden from the Nazis in a farmhouse by a Christian family. **J**

Renee Roth-Hanno. *Touch Wood: A Girlhood in Occupied France*. New York: Puffin Books, 1989.

The story of a "hidden child" who was brought up as a Catholic but reclaimed her Jewish identity after the war. **J**

Ruth Sender. *The Cage*. New York: Macmillan, 1986.

The dramatic account of a Polish Jewish girl's survival in the Lodz ghetto and Auschwitz. **J**

S. L. Shneiderman, editor. *Warsaw Ghetto: A Diary by Mary Berg*. New York: L. B. Fischer, 1945.

A first-hand account of life in the Warsaw ghetto, written by a 15-year-old. **HC**

Nechama Tec. *Dry Tears: The Story of a Lost Childhood*. New York: Oxford University Press, 1984.

The author and her family were Polish Jews who survived on the Aryan side of the ghetto. **HC**

Nelly S. Toll. *Behind the Secret Window: A Memoir of a Hidden Childhood*. New York: Dial Books, 1993.

Toll talks about her life in Lvov, Poland, before the war and her experiences hiding with her mother from the Nazis. The book reproduces watercolors that she painted during that period. **J**

Elie Wiesel. *Night*. New York: Bantam Books, 1982.

In one of the most widely read memoirs of the Holocaust, Wiesel provides a powerful account of his experience in Auschwitz– Birkenau. He arrived at the camp as a young boy and, after the Death March, he was liberated at Buchenwald. **JHC**

Ruth E. Wolman. *Crossing Over: An Oral History of Refugees From Hitler's Reich*. New York: Macmillan, 1996.

Memoirs of Austrian and German Jews who fled Europe between 1938 and 1941. **HC**

Survivors and the Generation After

Eleanor H. Ayer with Alfons Heck and Helen Waterford. *Parallel Journeys*. New York: Atheneum, 1995.

This book, a recipient of numerous literary awards, tells the personal stories of two individuals who experienced the Holocaust, from very different vantage points—Helen Waterford, a Jewish survivor of Auschwitz, and Alfons Heck, a former member of the Hitler Youth. **JHC**

Yehuda Bauer. *Flight and Rescue: Brichah. The Organized Escape of the Jewish Survivors of Eastern Europe, 1944–1948*. New York: Random House, 1970.

A detailed history of the mass movement of survivors by a clandestine underground organization. **HC**

Helen Epstein. *Children of the Holocaust: Conversations with Sons and Daughters of Survivors*. New York: Putnam, 1979.

The first book written for the general public on the "second generation." **C**

Martin Gilbert. *The Boys: The Story of 732 Young Concentration Camp Survivors*. New York: Henry Holt, 1997.

The experiences of these young men are told in their own words, through Gilbert's historical narrative. A powerful personal history of the Holocaust. **HC**

William Helmreich. *Against All Odds: Holocaust Survivors and the Lives They Made in America*. New York: Simon & Schuster, 1992.

The story of Holocaust survivors who learned to live and trust again. **HC**

Isabella Leitner. *Saving the Fragments: From Auschwitz to New York*. New York: New American Library, 1985.

A sequel to Fragments of Isabella *that traces the author's journey from liberation to the beginning of a new life.* **JHC**

Dorothy Rabinowitz. *New Lives: Survivors of the Holocaust Living in America.* New York: Alfred A. Knopf, 1976.

Personal stories of survivors of the Holocaust living in the United States. **HC**

An antisemitic caricature from the Viennese magazine *Kikeriki*, 1912.

Antisemitism

David Berger, editor. *History and Hate.* Philadelphia: The Jewish Publication Society, 1986.

Eight essays that analyze the dynamics of antisemitism as it has appeared through different periods of human history. **JHC**

Edward H. Flannery. *The Anguish of the Jews.* New York: Macmillan, 1965.

Father Flannery traces the history of antisemitism from the ancient world to the post-Holocaust world. **HC**

Jacob Katz. *From Prejudice to Destruction: Anti-Semitism 1700–1933.* Cambridge, MA: Harvard University Press, 1980.

Katz describes the process by which a set of negative ideas about the Jews were gradually transformed into a social force that led to their near-total destruction. **HC**

Charles Patterson. *Anti-Semitism: The Road to the Holocaust and Beyond.* New York: Walker and Company, 1988.

This book provides a history of antisemitism from ancient times in various parts of the world. **HC**

Leon Poliakov. *The History of Anti-Semitism: From Voltaire to Wagner.* New York: Vanguard Press, 1975.

This is the third volume in Poliakov's history of antisemitism. It traces antisemitism in the period from 1700 to 1870. **HC**

Leon Poliakov. *The History of Anti-Semitism: Suicidal Europe 1870–1933.* New York: Vanguard Press, 1985.

Leon Poliakov traces the development and spread of antisemitism throughout Europe in the crucial years leading up to the Holocaust. **HC**

Robert S. Wistrich. *Antisemitism: The Longest Hatred.* New York: Pantheon Books, 1991.

A comprehensive, well-written narrative of the history of anti-semitism, from its ancient roots to its present-day aspects. **HC**

Specialized Studies

Deborah Dwork. *Children with a Star: Jewish Youth in Nazi Europe.* New Haven, CT: Yale University Press, 1991.

A detailed study that looks at the daily life of Jewish young people during the Holocaust. **C**

A program bill from a night club in the Warsaw ghetto, circa 1940–1942.

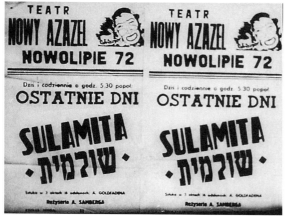

Gila Flam. *Singing for Survival: Songs of the Lodz Ghetto, 1940–1945.* Chicago: University of Illinois Press, 1992.

A detailed analysis of the rich musical culture that was created and performed in Poland's Lodz ghetto. **C**

Lawrence L. Langer. *Holocaust Testimonies: The Ruins of Memory.* New Haven, CT: Yale University Press, 1991.

A work analyzing the characteristics of oral history and its difference from written memoir. **C**

Deborah Lipstadt. *Denying the Holocaust: The Growing Assault on Truth and Memory.* New York: The Free Press, 1993.

An overview of the main figures involved in promoting the denial of the Holocaust in the United States and abroad and a look at their motives and methods. **C**

Jewish women are forced to shovel stones in the Radom ghetto, Poland, circa 1940.

Carol Rittner and John K. Roth, editors. *Different Voices: Women and the Holocaust.* New York: Paragon House, 1993.

An examination of women's experiences during the Holocaust. **C**

John K. Roth and Michael Berenbaum, editors. *The Holocaust: Religious and Philosophical Implications.* New York: Paragon House, 1989.

A collection of essays dealing with difficult questions about the Holocaust. **C**

Richard Rubenstein. *The Cunning of History.* New York: HarperCollins, 1987.

An extended essay that attempts to put the Holocaust into historical perspective. **C**

Illustrated Books

This brief listing includes collections of artwork that were created primarily by victims of the Holocaust to illustrate their experiences in the ghettos, concentration camps, and in hiding.

> **Key**
>
> **J** = grades 7–8
> **H** = grades 9–12
> **C** = college and above

Jane Blatter and Sybil Milton. *Art of the Holocaust*. New York: The Routledge Press, 1981.

This volume contains more than 350 pieces of artwork created by victims of the Nazis in ghettos, concentration camps, and in hiding. **HC**

Alexander Bogen. *Revolt*. Beit Lohamei Haghetaot, Israel, 1989.

This album presents a pictorial account of Jewish partisans during the Holocaust. **JHC**

Mary S. Costanza. *The Living Witness: Art in the Concentration Camps and Ghettos*. New York: Macmillan, 1982.

This record of remembrance presents 100 works of art from concentration camps and ghettos, ranging from small fragments to complete drawings. **HC**

Joseph P. Czarnecki. *Last Traces: The Lost Art of Auschwitz.* New York: Atheneum, 1989.

A collection of drawings and paintings that depicts life in Auschwitz–Birkenau. **HC**

Toby Fluek. *Memories of My Life in a Polish Village 1930–1949.* New York: Alfred A. Knopf, 1990.

A pictorial memoir of Fluek's life as a child growing up in a Polish village and her experiences during and after the Holocaust. **JHC**

Valentine Jacober Furth. *Cabbage & Geraniums: Memories of the Holocaust.* New York: Columbia University Press, 1989.

This volume describes the experiences of the author and her family during the Holocaust. **JHC**

Gerald Green. *The Artists of Terezin.* New York: Hawthorne Books, 1969.

This collection of paintings, drawings, and sketches that survived the Holocaust—many of the artists themselves did not—portrays life in Theresienstadt camp, memories of those left behind, and their hopes for the future. **HC**

Roberto Innocenti, *Rose Blanche.* Mankato, MN: Creative Education, Inc., 1985.

On one level, this volume appears to be a picture book intended for very young children. On another level, however, it is an artistic expression of the Holocaust as seen through the eyes of a child. It conveys the child's failure to understand or accept the events that took place around her. **JHC**

A Jewish boy sells armbands adorned with the Star of David in the streets of the Warsaw ghetto.

Alfred Kantor. *The Book of Alfred Kantor.* New York: Schocken Books, 1971.

Alfred Kantor composed this illustrated diary while at a Displaced Persons camp in 1945. The 160 drawings are a testimony of his experiences in the concentration camps. **JHC**

Sybil Milton, editor. *The Art of Jewish Children: Germany 1936–1941.* New York: Philosophical Library, 1989.

The 125 drawings in this collection were created by Jewish children in Germany in the segregated schools they were forced to attend. The drawings reveal their hopes and fears as they tried, through art, to find a way to transcend the horror of their experiences. **HC**

Miriam Novitsch. *Spiritual Resistance 1940–1945.* Philadelphia: The Jewish Publication Society, 1981.

A collection of the work of 48 artists from the ghettos and concentration camps. **JHC**

Vivian Alpert Thompson. *A Mission in Art.* Macon, GA: Mercer University Press, 1988.

This book deals with the work of American survivor-artists, "empathizers," and children of survivors who have made the Holocaust the focus of their work. **HC**

Hana Volavkova, editor. *I Never Saw Another Butterfly: Children's Drawings and Poems from Terezin Concentration Camp, 1942–1944.* New York: Schocken Books, 1993.

A collection of collages, drawings, and poems that serves as a poignant memorial to the children of Theresienstadt. **JHC**

C H A P T E R **3**

Videos

The Holocaust is one of the most—if not the most—documented event of modern history. The Germans kept an extensive photographic record of their activities during World War II. Those films and photographs have been preserved, enabling us to see much of what occurred. Those images, as well as those taken by Jews and others, allow us to trace the history of this tragic event.

> **Key**
>
> **J** = grades 7–8
> **H** = grades 9–12
> **C** = college and above

European Jewry Before the Holocaust

The Camera of My Family

The history of one German family is portrayed through four generations, from 1845 to 1945. The photographs are, for the most part, real portraits of the family of Catherine Noren, a professional photographer.

Specifications: 18 minutes. Color & BW. VHS filmstrip. Date released: 1977. **JHC**

Topics: antisemitism; prejudice; rise of Nazism

Available from: Anti-Defamation League of B'nai B'rith, (800) 343-5540

Young Berta Rosenhein Hertz plays in the garden of her home in Leipzig, Germany, 1928.

Echoes That Remain

A poignant study of Jewish *shtetl* life before the Holocaust, this video combines hundreds of rare archival photos and previously unseen footage with live-action sequences shot on location at the sites of former Jewish communities in Czechoslovakia, Hungary, Poland, and Romania.

Specifications: 60 minutes. Color. VHS. Date produced: 1991. **JHC**

Topics: Eastern Europe; Jewish society; *shtetls*

Available from: Simon Wiesenthal Center, (310) 553-9036

Images Before My Eyes

This film re-creates Jewish life in Poland from the late 1800s to the 1930s, a unique and now-vanished era. With rare film footage, photographs, memorabilia, music, and interviews, this film brings to life the full range of the Jewish experience in the years before the Holocaust.

Specifications: 90 minutes. Color & BW. VHS. **JHC**

Topic: Jewish life in pre-World War II Poland

Available from: many libraries and Holocaust resource centers

Sighet, Sighet

Nobel laureate Elie Wiesel revisits Sighet, the town of his childhood in Transylvania (Romania). In 1944, he and his family were deported by the Nazis to Auschwitz–Birkenau along with the Jews of the ghetto. Wiesel movingly and poetically narrates the search of his past in a town that was once, but is no longer, a center of Jewish life.

Specifications: 30 minutes. BW. VHS. Date released: 1968. **JHC**

Topics: Sighet; Elie Wiesel

Available from: Alden Films; many libraries and Holocaust resource centers

The Holocaust: A General Overview

Children in the Holocaust

Depicting the plight of Jewish children during the Holocaust from the viewpoint of the now-grown survivors, this film is a candid and personal account of the terrors of the period, as seen through the eyes of children.

Specifications: 70 minutes. Color & BW. VHS. Date released: 1989. **JHC**

Topics: children of the Holocaust; survivors

Available from: Phoenix Films & Video Inc.

Genocide (Story of Man's Inhumanity to Man)

This film, produced by the Simon Wiesenthal Center, uses documentary film footage and photographs along with moving narration by Orson Welles and Elizabeth Taylor to provide one of the best introductions to the subject of genocide. It is recommended for audiences who are unfamiliar with the subject as well as for knowledgeable viewers.

Specifications: 90 minutes. Color. VHS. Date produced: 1981. **JHC**

Topics: Final Solution; genocide; Holocaust history

Available from: Simon Wiesenthal Center, (310) 553-9036

Witness to the Holocaust

This film consists of seven different segments, each covering a different aspect of the Holocaust, from the rise of the Nazis to liberation.

Specifications: 7 segments, 10 to 15 minutes each. BW. VHS. **JHC**

Topic: Holocaust

Available from: Anti-Defamation League of B'nai B'rith, (800) 343-5540

Germany, Hitler, and the Rise of Nazism

Hitler: Anatomy of a Dictatorship

This documentary, featuring archival and newsreel footage, depicts the rise to power of Adolf Hitler and the Nazi Party from the 1920s through World War II.
Specifications: 23 minutes. BW. VHS. Copyright 1969. **JHC**
Topics: Adolf Hitler; Nazism
Available from: Social Studies School Service, (800) 421-4246

Hitler—The Whole Story: The Early Years

This film, the first part of a documentary trilogy about Hitler's career, focuses on his early years, examining the factors behind his rise to power.
Specifications: 50 minutes. Color & BW. VHS. Copyright 1989. **JHC**
Topics: antisemitism; prejudice; rise of Nazism
Available from: Social Studies School Service, (800) 421-4246

Hitler—The Whole Story: The Rise of the Reich

The second part of a documentary trilogy about Hitler's career, this film examines his consolidation of power and his buildup of the Nazi totalitarian state.
Specifications: 50 minutes. Color & BW. VHS. Copyright 1989. **JHC**
Topics: Adolf Hitler; Third Reich; totalitarian state
Available from: Social Studies School Service, (800) 421-4246

Hitler—The Whole Story: The War Years

The third part of a documentary trilogy about Hitler's career, this film concentrates on the Nazi military strategy during World War II as well as on the genocidal atrocities perpetrated by the Nazis.
Specifications: 50 minutes. Color & BW. VHS. Copyright 1989. **JHC**
Topics: genocide; Adolf Hitler; World War II
Available from: Social Studies School Service, (800) 421-4246

Hitler's Germany (1933–1936)

Started as a small group in the 1920s, Hitler and the Nazi Party manged to take control of Germany by 1933 through political persecution and violence. The film describes the pre-war period, the subsequent reoccupation of the Rhineland in 1936, the persecution of the Jews, and the growth of the Nazi propaganda machine under Josef Goebbels.

Specifications: 20 minutes. BW. VHS film. Date released: 1983. **JHC**

Topics: history; Adolf Hitler; rise of Nazism

Available from: Films, Inc. (Chicago), (800) 826-3456

How the Nazis Came to Power

This film analyzes the social, economic, political, and psychological forces at work in Germany after its defeat and humiliation in World War I. This insight helps to explain the appeal and success of Nazism and how the Nazis' message found willing followers among the German people.

Specifications: 17 minutes. BW. VHS. Date released: 1990. **JHC**

Topics: Nazism; Weimar Republic

Available from: Films for the Humanities & Sciences, (800) 257-5126

Make Germany Pay

A portrait of life in Germany after its defeat in World War I. The Armistice Agreement and the Treaty of Versailles triggered widespread anger among the German people and helped to prepare them for the eventual rise of Nazism. This film deals with the financial inflation and the problems caused by French and Belgian occupation of the Ruhr.

Specifications: 20 minutes. BW. VHS. Copyright 1989. **JHC**

Topic: rise of Nazism

Available from: Films, Inc. (Chicago), (800) 826-3456

The Making of the German Nation

A vivid account of German history from the creation of the German Empire following the defeat of Napoleon Bonaparte to the rise of Nazism and World War II.
Specifications: 94 minutes. BW. VHS. **HC**
Topic: German history
Available from: Educational Audio Visual Inc., (914) 769-6332

The Master Race

This video shows how and why the Nazi concept of racial superiority developed and how the German nation was organized to put this idea into action. The film focuses on the 1936 Berlin Olympic Games as grist for the government propaganda mill and looks at organized persecution as an element of government policy.
Specifications: 20 minutes. BW. VHS. Date released: 1983. **JHC**
Topics: history of Nazism; Nazi racial theories; 1936 Olympics
Available from: Films for the Humanities & Sciences, (800) 257-5126

The Nazi Seizure of Power

This film traces the rise of Nazi power from the Reichstag (German Parliament) seats won by the Nazis in the election of 1930 to the appointment of Adolf Hitler as chancellor and the death of Paul von Hindenburg.
Specifications: 33 minutes. BW. VHS. **JHC**
Topic: history of Nazism in Germany
Available from: many libraries and Holocaust resource centers

A New Germany 1933–1939

Volume 1 of *The World at War* series, narrated by Sir Laurence Olivier. Embittered by its defeat in World War I and stricken by economic depression, Germany rallies to the new hope promised by the Nazis. Book-burning and anti-Jewish legislation ensue.
Specifications: 52 minutes. BW. VHS. **JHC**
Topic: history of Nazism in Germany
Available from: many libraries and Holocaust resource centers

The Rise and Fall of Adolf Hitler

A comprehensive documentary about Hitler that looks in detail at his career and motivations. The film examines the economic, psychological, political, and social forces as well as the consequences of Hitler's regime.

Specifications: 150 minutes. BW. VHS. Date released: 1989. **JHC**

Topics: Adolf Hitler; Nazi Germany; Third Reich

Available from: Films for the Humanities & Sciences, (800) 257-5126

Ghettos

A Field of Buttercups

The story of Dr. Janusz Korczak's orphanage for Jewish children in the Warsaw ghetto and his heroic devotion to the orphans.

Specifications: 30 minutes. BW. VHS. Date released: 1969. **JHC**

Topics: children; Janusz Korczak; Warsaw ghetto

Available from: Alden Films; many libraries and Holocaust resource centers

Lodz Ghetto

Ordinary people confide what they felt during the darkest days of Nazi persecution in Poland. Scripted entirely from the secret diaries left behind by ghetto residents, this film dramatically reveals the struggle of 200,000 people against the seemingly unstoppable effort to crush them.

Specifications: 118 minutes. Color & BW. VHS. Date released: 1993. **JHC**

Topics: Lodz ghetto; Poland

Available from: Filmic Archives, (203) 261-1920

The Story of Chaim Rumkowski and the Jews of Lodz

In order to facilitate the destruction of Poland's Jews—approximately 3.3 million before the war—the Germans forced them to establish *Judenrate* ("Jewish Councils"). Chaim Rumkowski, who was appointed by the Nazis as chairman of the Lodz *Judenrat*, was responsible for all administrative and social services within the ghetto. Rumkowski attempted to turn the Lodz ghetto into an industrial center, but his strategy for survival was doomed to failure.

Specifications: 55 minutes. Color. VHS. Copyright 1982. **JHC**
Topics: *Judenrate*; Lodz ghetto; Chaim Rumkowski
Available from: The Cinema Guild, (212) 246-5522

The Warsaw Ghetto

Based on a compilation of Nazi photographic records, this film depicts the Warsaw ghetto from its creation in 1940 until its destruction in 1943. It shows the daily lives of Jews within the ghetto and their struggle to maintain their cultural and religious identity and their dignity. It includes scenes of atrocity and starvation.

Specifications: 51 minutes. BW. VHS. Copyright 1969. **HC**
Topics: Nazi atrocities; Warsaw ghetto
Available from: Social Studies School Service, (800) 421-4246

Concentration and Extermination Camps

Camp of Hope and Despair—Witnesses of Westerbork

Westerbork, in eastern Holland, was the last stop on Dutch soil for more than 100,000 Dutch Jews before they were deported to the concentration camps. Despite the air of impending doom, Jewish classes, celebrations, religious services, and weddings were held there on a regular basis. Through the eyewitness accounts of survivors as well as remarkable photographs and film footage, one comes to understand the overall picture of daily life in the transit camp. Voice-over narrative.

Specifications: 70 minutes. Color. VHS. Date released: 1995. **JHC**
Topics: Dutch Jews; Holland; spiritual resistance; Westerbork
Available from: Ergo Media Inc., (201) 692-0404

The Death Camps

Part of a learning package that includes a variety of resource materials for teaching the Holocaust. It contains historical footage, still photos, background information, and commentary from former *New York Times* executive editor A. M. Rosenthal. Holocaust survivor and author Elie Wiesel is also featured.
Specifications: 70 minutes. Color. VHS. Date released: 1995. **JHC**
Topics: Auschwitz–Birkenau; Buchenwald; concentration camps; Dachau; death camps; ghettos
Available from: Educational Media, (212) 499-3300

Drancy: A Concentration Camp in Paris, 1941-1944

Details the complicity of French authorities during German occupation in arresting and interning more than 74,000 Jews prior to their transport to Auschwitz–Birkenau. It highlights the role of the French in rounding up the Jews and of instituting antisemitic laws on its own initiative. Features interviews with survivors and bystanders as well as rare archival footage.
Specifications: 55 minutes. BW. VHS. Date released: 1995. **JHC**
Topics: antisemitism; Drancy, France; Vichy, France
Available from: Filmmakers Library, (212) 808-4980

After liberation in May 1945, German civilians from Nammering were forced to bury the corpses of prisoners who had been shot by the SS.

Kitty—Return to Auschwitz

Kitty Hart, a Holocaust survivor who lived in Auschwitz between the ages of 16 and 18, returns to the camp to tell others about her experiences there.
Specifications: 82 minutes. Color. VHS. Date released: 1979. **HC**
Topics: Auschwitz; survivors
Available from: Social Studies School Service, (800) 421-4246

Paradise Camp

A documentary about Theresienstadt camp in Czechoslovakia, which was built by the Nazis as a transit camp for Jews bound for extermination camps like Auschwitz–Birkenau. The film features survivors who tell of their experiences.
Specifications: 56 minutes. Color & BW. VHS. Copyright 1986. **JHC**
Topics: ghettos; survivors; Theresienstadt
Available from: The Cinema Guild, Inc., (212) 246-5522

Terezin Diary

In 1941, the Nazis converted Terezin, an old fortress town near Prague, Czechoslovakia, into a concentration camp for Jews. The Nazis intended to use this "model" camp, as they called it, for propaganda purposes. In reality, Theresienstadt (the camp, as opposed to the town, Terezin) was a way station to extermination camps in the east, and the more than 200,000 prisoners who passed through the camp, including some 15,000 children, lived in hideously overcrowded barracks, facing hunger, disease, and the constant threat of deportation to Auschwitz–Birkenau. At least 33,000 people died in Terezin. This film tells the story of the ghetto and its children.
Specifications: 99 minutes. Color. VHS. Date released: 1993. **JHC**
Topics: children; Czechoslovakia; Terezin/Theresienstadt
Available from: Ergo Media Inc., (201) 692-0404

Theresienstadt—Gateway to Auschwitz

Survivors of Theresienstadt who were children during the war tell their stories. The live film footage is interspersed with original artwork and photographs. Approximately 15,000 children under the age of 15 were incarcerated in Theresienstadt; only about 100 of them are known to have survived.
Specifications: 60 minutes. Color & BW. VHS. **JHC**
Topics: children; Holocaust art; Terezin/Theresienstadt
Available from: The Cinema Guild, (212) 246-5522

The Triumph of Memory

This film is about non-Jewish resistance fighters who were sent to concentration camps during World War II. They bear witness to the Holocaust and serve as a moving reminder of the Nazis' actions in Mauthausen, Buchenwald, and Auschwitz–Birkenau. The film is narrated by Arnost Lustig, a Jewish survivor of Auschwitz and twice winner of the National Jewish Book Award.

Specifications: 29 minutes. Color & BW. VHS. Date released: 1989. **HC**

Topics: concentration camps; resistance; Righteous Gentiles

Available from: PBS Video, (800) 344-3337

Resistance

Forest of Valor

This film documents the story of Jewish underground fighters and partisans who fought the German Army in the forests of Eastern Europe during World War II.

Specifications: 52 minutes. Color. VHS. Date released: 1995. **JHC**

Topics: Babi Yar; partisans; resistance

Available from: many libraries and Holocaust resource centers

The Little Soldiers

Jewish partisans of World War II who fought in the forests of Poland, Lithuania, and White Russia (present-day Belarus) during World War II meet in an Israeli forest to reminisce about their wartime experiences.

Specifications: 14 minutes. Color & BW. VHS. Date released: 1988. **JHC**

Topic: resistance

Available from: Alden Films; many libraries and Holocaust resource centers

Not Like Sheep to the Slaughter

In the summer of 1943, a small group of resistance fighters, led by 24-year-old Mordechai Tenenbaum, attempted to thwart the Nazi plan to eradicate the Bialystok ghetto. With few weapons and little outside assistance, these fighters resisted the Nazis with incredible resolve. In light of newly uncovered evidence from that period, survivors and witnesses, among them former Israeli Knesset (Parliament) member Haika Grossman, provide keen insight into one of the lesser-known acts of courage displayed by the Jewish resistance movement during the Holocaust.
Specifications: 150 minutes. BW. VHS. Date released: 1991. **JHC**
Topics: Bialystok ghetto; resistance
Available from: Ergo Home Video, (201) 692-0404

Partisans of Vilna

This documentary explores Jewish resistance in Lithuania during World War II. It recounts the moral dilemmas faced by Jewish youths who organized an underground resistance in the Vilnius (Vilna) ghetto and fought as partisans in the woods against the Nazis. The film features interviews in Hebrew, Yiddish, and English with the former partisans in Israel, New York City, Montreal, and Vilnius. It includes rare archival footage from 1939 to 1944. English subtitles.
Specifications: 130 minutes. Color & BW. VHS. **JHC**
Topics: resistance; Vilnius (Vilna)
Available from: many libraries and Holocaust resource centers

Warsaw Ghetto

This tape describes the Holocaust and, in particular, events that occurred in 1943 in Warsaw, Poland.
Specifications: 20 minutes. BW. VHS. **JHC**
Topics: resistance; Warsaw ghetto
Available from: Jewish Labor Committee, (212) 477-0707

Warsaw Ghetto Uprising

In commemoration of the 50th anniversary of the Warsaw ghetto uprising, this video was produced by the Ghetto Fighters' House at Kibbutz Lohamei Hagetaot, Israel. Archival film footage, photographs, and testimonies of survivors provide insight into the event. Beginning with the Nazi invasion of Poland, viewers are led through the deportations, life in the ghetto, the formation of a resistance organization, and, finally, the uprising. English narration.

Specifications: 23 minutes. Color & BW. VHS. Date released: 1993. **JHC**

Topics: resistance; Warsaw ghetto uprising

Available from: Ergo Media Inc., (201) 692-0404

Rescue

As If It Were Yesterday

This film documents the heroism of the Belgian people who, during the German occupation of Belgium, helped more than 4,000 Jewish children to hide or to escape deportation and extermination, often at the risk of their own lives.

Specifications: 85 minutes. BW. VHS. Date released: 1985. **JHC**

Topics: Belgium; hiding children; Righteous Gentiles

Available from: many libraries and Holocaust resource centers

The Avenue of the Just

The title refers to the tree-lined walk at Yad Vashem, Israel's Holocaust memorial, honoring the Righteous Gentiles who saved Jews. The film features interviews with men and women who made such sacrifices and with some of the people they saved.

Specifications: 58 minutes. Color. VHS. **JHC**

Topic: Righteous Gentiles

Available from: many libraries and Holocaust resource centers

The Children from Villa Emma

This docudrama re-creates the rescue of a group of Jewish children from the Nazis by Righteous Gentiles of a small village in northern Italy. Shot on location, the film incorporates actors, rare archival footage, and moving interviews with the survivors. Hebrew with English subtitles.

Specifications: 50 minutes. Color & BW. VHS. Date released: 1982. **JHC**

Topics: children; Italy; Righteous Gentiles

Available from: Israel Video; many libraries and Holocaust resource centers

Courage to Care

An encounter with ordinary people who refused to succumb to Nazi tyranny. They followed their consciences while most others "followed orders." They fed strangers, kept secrets, and provided hiding places. Their actions were exceptional in an era marked by apathy and complicity.

Specifications: 28 minutes. Color & BW. VHS, 16 mm. Date released: 1986. **JHC**

Topic: Righteous Gentiles

Available from: Anti-Defamation League of B'nai B'rith, (800) 343-5540

A Debt to Honor

A documentary video that tells the compelling stories of ordinary individuals whose personal acts of courage resulted in the rescue of thousands of Jews after the Germans occupied Italy in 1943.

Specifications: 30 minutes. Color. VHS. Date released: 1995. **JHC**

Topics: Italy; rescue; Righteous Gentiles

Available from: Documentaries International Film and Video Foundation, (202) 429-9320

Jacoba

While Anne Frank and her family were hidden in an attic in Amsterdam, another Jewish family was similarly sheltered in a small Dutch village. But, unlike the Franks, this family survived. The Ten Brinks were saved by an extraordinary Christian woman, Jacoba Omvlee, who hid them in a tiny attic in her windmill. For three years, this devout Calvinist risked her own life and the lives of her eight children to defy the Germans and local Dutch collaborators.
Specifications: 63 minutes. Color. VHS. Date released: 1989. **JHC**
Topics: Holland; Righteous Gentiles
Available from: Filmmakers Library, (212) 808-4980

Missing Hero

Swedish diplomat Raoul Wallenberg risked his life to save at least 100,000 Hungarian Jews from the Nazi gas chambers. He then disappeared mysteriously in 1945, under Soviet military escort. The Soviets never fully explained his fate, but evidence suggests that he may have survived the war. Former Israeli prime minister Menachem Begin called Wallenberg the "greatest hero of World War II."
Specifications: 50 minutes. Color & BW. VHS. Date released: 1984. **JHC**
Topics: Hungary; Righteous Gentiles; Raoul Wallenberg
Available from: Films Incorporated Video, (800) 826-3456

Raoul Wallenberg: Buried Alive

This film reconstructs the story of the young Swedish diplomat who saved the lives of at least 100,000 Jews before his disappearance. It includes archival material showing the rise of the Arrow Cross Nazis in Hungary and footage of ghetto pogroms and death marches. Also included are interviews with survivors who were saved by Wallenberg and with those who reported seeing him alive.

Specifications: 58 minutes. Color. VHS. Date released: 1984. **JHC**
Topics: rescue; Righteous Gentiles; Raoul Wallenberg
Available from: Direct Cinema Ltd. (Los Angeles), (310) 636-8200

Rescue in Scandinavia

This video focuses on the courageous acts of Christian rescuers who guided thousands of Jews to safety in Sweden. Narrated by Swedish actress Liv Ullmann, it recounts the role of the government and citizens of Sweden in providing sanctuary for Jewish refugees. The film also details the rescue assignment of Raoul Wallenberg with the assistance of Per Anger, tells about the role of Finland's Ambassador Max Jakobson in the rescue program, and pays tribute to the citizens of Denmark and Norway who saved the lives of their Jewish countrymen.
Specifications: 55 minutes. Color & BW. VHS. Date released: 1994. **JHC**
Topics: Denmark; Finland; Norway; rescuers; Righteous Gentiles; Sweden
Available from: Documentaries International Film and Video Foundation, (202) 429-9320

The Righteous Enemy

This documentary reveals one of the most remarkable yet little-known rescue operations of the Holocaust: the active protection given to approximately 40,000 Jews in occupied France, Greece, and Yugoslavia by Italian military and government officials.
Specifications: 84 minutes. Color & BW. VHS. Date released: 1987. **JHC**
Topics: Jews under Italian occupation; rescue
Available from: The National Center for Jewish Film, (617) 899-7044

Weapons of the Spirit

This film by Pierre Sauvage tells the true story of Le Chambon, a small French village whose inhabitants saved some 5,000 Jews during the Holocaust. The people of Le Chambon are descendants of Huguenots, Protestants who were persecuted for their religious beliefs in previous centuries. They decided to resist evil with the "weapons of the spirit" and managed to double the population of their community right under the Nazis' noses. This is Sauvage's personal story, as he was born to Jewish parents hiding in Le Chambon. He returned and interviewed the villagers for this work.

Specifications: 90 minutes. Color. VHS. Date released: 1989. **JHC**
Topics: Le Chambon, France; rescue; Righteous Gentiles
Available from: Chambon Foundation, Pierre Sauvage, president, (213) 650-1774

Other Victims of Nazi Persecution

Jehovah's Witnesses Stand Firm Against Nazi Assault

Featuring 10 historians from Europe and North America and more than 20 Jehovah's Witness survivors, this documentary tells the story of the persecution of Witnesses by the Nazi regime.

Specifications: 78 minutes. Color & BW. VHS. **JHC**
Topic: Jehovah's Witnesses
Available from: Watchtower Bible and Tract Society of New York, (718) 625-3600

Persecuted & Forgotten (The Gypsies of Auschwitz)

This tape follows a group of German Romani (Gypsies) as they return to Auschwitz–Birkenau to come to terms with their experiences under the Nazi regime. Through moving personal accounts, individuals tell about the "Gypsy Police," the Institute of Racial Hygiene, and the doctor responsible for genealogical research, leading to their imprisonment and liquidation. Many of the Romani interviewed in this eye-opening documentary address the discrimination they still experience today.

Specifications: 54 minutes. Color. VHS. Date released: 1989. **JHC**

Topic: Romani
Available from: EBS Productions, (415) 495-2327

We Were Marked with a Big "A"

This video tells the story of three gay Holocaust surviviors. The name of the film refers to a yellow cloth with a big "A" on it that some victims were initially forced to wear around their legs. Later, when the camp marking system became more developed, all homosexual inmates were forced to wear a pink triangle. In German, with English subtitles.
Specifications: 44 minutes. Color & BW. VHS. Date released: 1994. **C**
Topic: Homosexuals
Available from: United States Holocaust Memorial Museum, (202) 488-6144

Liberation

In Their Words

This award-winning tape contains excerpts from interviews of Holocaust survivors and American soldiers who participated in the liberation of the death camps during World War II.
Specifications: 30 minutes. Color & BW. VHS. Date released: 1983. **JHC**
Topics: death camps; liberators; survivors
Available from: Southeastern Florida Holocaust Memorial Center, (305) 919-5690

The Liberation of KZ Dachau

This documentary chronicles the personal stories of the soldiers who first entered the concentration camp at Dachau on April 29, 1945. They were so overwhelmed by the horrors they found that the battle-hardened soldiers broke down in front of the camp's

remaining prisoners. This story tells how one event brought home the true meaning of the war and why so many fought and died.
Specifications: 94 minutes. Color. VHS. Date released: 1990. **JHC**
Topics: concentration camps; Dachau; liberation
Available from: Strong Communications; many libraries and Holocaust resource centers

You Are Free

This film features interviews with five people who were present when the camps were liberated—four Americans who helped in the liberation and one woman who survived the camps. Rare footage of the camps from the United States National Archives is included.
Specifications: 20 minutes. Color & BW. VHS. Date released: 1984. **JHC**
Topics: liberation; survivors
Available from: Direct Cinema Ltd. (Los Angeles), (310) 636-8200

Memoirs

Born in Berlin

This documentary is about three young girls who called Berlin home during the 1930s, until Nazi laws against Jews shattered their lives. Filmed on location in Germany, Sweden, Bulgaria, and Israel, the film traces their lives from pre-war Berlin through the traumas of war and its aftermath.
Specifications: 85 minutes. BW. VHS. Date released: 1991. **JHC**
Topic: survivors
Available from: The National Center for Jewish Film, (617) 899-7044

Chasing Shadows

After 45 years, Hugo Gryn returns to his hometown, Berehovo, in Carpathia—once part of Czechoslovakia and, until the making of this film, closed to visitors from the Western world. This film provides a glimpse of a time when half the population of Berehovo were Jewish. It evokes the world of Gryn's childhood—a world that has all but vanished, leaving only ghosts and shadows.

Specifications: 52 minutes. Color & BW. VHS. Date released: 1990. **JHC**

Topics: Czechoslovakia; pre-Holocaust Jewish life

Available from: The National Center for Jewish Film, (617) 899-7044

Diamonds in the Snow

Three women born in Bendzin, Poland, recall a childhood of hiding from the Nazis and talk about the Polish Christians who saved their lives. Of the thousands of Jewish children living in this Polish city at the time of the German invasion, barely a dozen survived the war. The story of this vanished community, conveyed through interviews and archival film and photos, forms a tragic counterpoint to the survival of these few children and the bravery of those Jews and Gentiles responsible for saving their lives.

Specifications: 59 minutes. Color & BW. VHS. Copyright 1994. **JHC**

Topics: Bendzin, Poland; children in hiding; Righteous Gentiles

Available from: The Cinema Guild, (212) 246-5522

Father's Return to Auschwitz

Jan Drabek, the son of an upper middle-class Christian family, lived in Prague before World War II. In 1938, when Germany occupied Czechoslovakia, his father joined the underground. Denounced and arrested, Jan's father was sent to the Auschwitz–Birkenau death camp, which he miraculously survived. Four decades later, he returned to the camp with his son Jan, who filmed this documentary. The film recalls the Nazi takeover of Czechoslovakia and the horrors of Auschwitz–Birkenau.

Specifications: 20 minutes. Color & BW. VHS. **JHC**
Topics: Auschwitz–Birkenau; Czechoslovakia; resistance
Available from: many libraries and Holocaust resource centers

A Journey Back

A personal documentary of Jack Garfein, a Holocaust survivor and Broadway producer, relating his experiences during World War II. He visits his former family home in Bardejov (formerly Czechoslovakia) as well as Auschwitz–Birkenau, the camp from which he was the only member of his family to survive.
Specifications: 60 minutes. Color & BW. VHS. **JHC**
Topics: Auschwitz–Birkenau; Czechoslovakia; survivors
Available from: Social Studies School Service, (800) 421-4246

Journey to Prague

In 1939, Nazi encroachment forced Otto Lowy to leave his home in Prague, Czechoslovakia. He never saw his family again. This film documents Lowy's return to his native city in 1987 and gives eloquent testimony to the Holocaust's power to haunt its survivors.
Specifications: 28 minutes. Color. VHS. **JHC**
Topics: Prague, Czechoslovakia; survivors
Available from: many libraries and Holocaust resource centers

One Survivor Remembers: The Gerda Weissman Klein Story

Jointly produced by Home Box Office and the United States Holocaust Memorial Museum. This is the story of liberation told through the memories of Holocaust survivor Gerda Weissman Klein. Her story conveys the creeping terror and devastating tragedy experienced by the millions who suffered under the Nazi regime. The film earned an Oscar for "Best Short Documentary," an Emmy, and a Cable Ace Award. Co-producers Michael Berenbaum and Raye Farr.
Specifications: 38 minutes. Color. VHS. Date released: 1995. **JHC**

Topics: survivors
Available from: United States Holocaust Memorial Museum,
(202) 488-0400

Return to My Shtetl *Delatyn*

This video chronicles Berl Nachim Lindwer's return to Galicia in
search of his *shtetl*, Delatyn, more than sixty years after he left.
Lindwer wanted to find out what happened to his family, who had
been murdered in the Holocaust. He also wanted to see the house
where he grew up and walk the streets of his beloved *shtetl*. Unique
film of pre-war *shtetl* life is juxtaposed with footage of Lindwer's
emotional pilgrimage. English and Dutch with English subititles.
Specifications: 60 minutes. Color. VHS. Date released: 1995. **JHC**
Topics: Bolechov; Cracow; Delatyn; Galicia; Lvov; Przemysl;
shtetl life; Stryz; survivor
Available from: Ergo Media Inc., (201) 692-0404

Robert Clary: A5714—A Memory of Liberation

Clary, who later starred in the television show "Hogan's Heroes,"
survived the Holocaust. This film documents his return to the
streets of Paris, to the railway lines of eastern Germany, and to
the Buchenwald concentration camp to retrace his tragic odyssey.
Specifications: 60 minutes. Color. VHS. **JHC**
Topics: concentration camps; survivors
Available from: many libraries and Holocaust resource centers

Tsvi Nussbaum—A Boy from Warsaw

This film tells the story behind the famous photograph of a
young boy standing with his arms raised, gazing into the camera.
The child in the picture—today a medical doctor living in New
York State—relates his experiences.
Specifications: 50 minutes. BW. VHS. **JHC**
Topics: children; Warsaw ghetto
Available from: MTV Finland; many libraries and Holocaust
resource centers

C H A P T E R **4**

Web Sites and CD-ROMs

This is an area that is just beginning to develop. In the next few years, many more Web sites will be created and perhaps hundreds of CD-ROMs will be produced.

Many individual Holocaust centers have Web sites that provide information about their organizations. For further information, see Chapter 5.

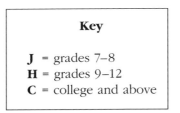

Key

J = grades 7–8
H = grades 9–12
C = college and above

Web Sites

- The United States Holocaust Memorial Museum homepage:
  http://www.ushmm.org
  This site provides a table of contents to guide the online user to the vast amount of information and resources available through this Web site and at the museum. Some major topics include the many museum facilities, guidelines for teaching the Holocaust, historical summaries, a videography for educators, answers to frequently asked questions about the Holocaust, daily life during the Holocaust, pre- and post- Holocaust life, a listing of Holocaust

resource centers in the United States, and a searchable database of the museum's archives and library that allows questions about specific subjects to be asked. **JHC**

- The homepage of Yad Vashem, Israel's museum and memorial to the victims of the Holocaust:
http://www.yad-vashem.org.il

This site is being developed and will, in time, be a major source of information on the Holocaust, including discussion of current Holocaust-related issues. **JHC**

- The Simon Wiesenthal Center homepage:
http://www.wiesenthal.com

This site contains answers to frequently asked questions about the Holocaust, biographies of children who experienced the Holocaust, updates on current events, information on hate groups on the Internet, and information about the center and the Museum of Tolerance in Los Angeles, California. Much of this information is available in several languages besides English, including Spanish, German, and Italian. **JHC**

- For general history, contact the homepage of the Cybrary of the Holocaust:
http://www.remember.org

One of the largest Web sites on the Holocaust, this contains a huge body of information, including answers to frequently asked questions, curriculum outlines, excerpts from survivor testimony, transcripts of Nazi speeches and official documents, artifact photos, historical photos, artwork, poetry, books written by survivors, links to other Holocaust Web sites, and genealogy-tracing information. Audio clips and transcripts of survivor testimony and interviews with scholars are available as well as a photo tour of Auschwitz–Birkenau. This site continues to grow. **JHC**

- The Anne Frank House:
  http://www.channels.nl/annefran.html

  This site currently includes a brief overview of Anne Frank's history and information about visiting the Secret Annexe at the house. The site is linked to a tour of Amsterdam, Holland. **JHC**

- An Auschwitz Alphabet:
  http://www.spectacle.org/695/ausch.html

  This personal and creative Web site is dedicated to Primo Levi, the well-known chemist, writer, and survivor of Auschwitz. The site gives a general overview of the Holocaust mainly through excerpts from memoirs and scholarly works, particularly those of Levi. It also includes links to other Holocaust-related sites. **JHC**

- L'Chaim: A Holocaust Web Project:
  http://www.charm.net/~rbennett/l'chaim.htmll

  Still under development, L'Chaim plans to become one of the major Web sites on the Holocaust. It includes a virtual tour of Dachau, excerpts from a survivor's story, and links to other Holocaust-related sites. Note: This site contains material that may disturb younger children. **JHC**

- Demonization of the Jew and the Jew as "Other": A Selected Bibliography:
  http://www3.huji.ac.il/www_jcd/dem.html

  Prepared for the international conference "The 'Other' as Threat: Demonization of Antisemitism," convened by the Vidal Sassoon International Center for the Study of the Holocaust at The Hebrew University of Jerusalem, Israel. The site provides an extensive list of titles on antisemitism from ancient times and in a variety of regions and cultures. **JHC**

- The Wannsee Conference Protocol:
  http://library.byu.edu/~rdh/eurodocs/germ/wanneng.html

  This site contains both English- and German-language transcriptions of the Wannsee Conference Protocol outlining the Nazi plan to exterminate the Jews of Europe. **JHC**

- Rescuers and Rescues:
  http://www.cs.cmu.edu/afs/cs.cmu.edu/user/mmbt/www/rescuers.html

  This site provides a long bibliography about rescuers and rescues during the Holocaust. **JHC**

- Southern Institute for Education and Research at Tulane University:
  http://www.Tulane.EDU/~so-inst/

  This site highlights anti-bias education resources for combating prejudice. It includes information about diversity training, Holocaust and civil education and lesson plans (including an online lesson plan on the movie Schindler's List*), transcripts of*

Residents of the Lodz ghetto in Poland bake matzah in preparation for Passover, 1940. This was the only year in which matzah was baked in the ghetto.

Holocaust-survivor testimony, and links to other sites dealing with civil rights, human rights, the Holocaust, Judaism and Jewish history, and African-American history and culture. **JHC**

- Ethical, Legal, and Political Sites on the Web homepage: ***http://www.spectacle.org/links.html***

  This site presents an annotated list of hotlinks to many Holocaust-related web sites. There are topics ranging from Bosnia, to civil rights and race, to the Holocaust, euthanasia, and religion. **JHC**

- Human Rights Internet: ***http://www.hri.ca***

  Provides much information on human rights. There are links to many legal documents, including the UN Convention on Genocide at: http:/www.traveller.com/~hrweb/legal/genocide.html. **JHC**

CD-ROMs

- ***Historical Atlas of the Holocaust***. Produced by the United States Holocaust Memorial Museum. From Macmillan Reference Library, (202) 488-6144

  This CD contains 275 full-color maps that present a visual survey of the Holocaust, 120 articles that place the maps in their historical context, more than 500 photos illustrating the geographic or thematic content of the maps, navigation aids (for example, theme and area listings), a detailed index, a map list, and map-to-map links. **JHC**

- ***Return to Life***. Produced by Yad Vashem, 972-2-6751611 (Israel).

  The first CD in an important series to be produced on the Holocaust. The story of survivors from liberation, it is a multimedia production, containing maps, films, photographs, interviews, and textual material. A teacher's manual is included. ***JHC***

Museums and Resource Centers

Each of the institutions listed in this section provides a unique variety of resources, programs, and services. For further information, contact each institution directly.

Australia

Jewish Holocaust Museum and Research Centre

13 Selwyn Street
Elstenwick
Melbourne, Victoria 3185
Australia
phone: (03) 9528-1985
fax: (03) 9528-3758

Sydney Jewish Museum

148 Darlinghurst Road
Darlinghurst
New South Wales 2010
Australia
phone: (02) 9360-7999
fax: (02) 9331-4245
e-mail: cohenj@tmx.com.au

Canada

The Montreal Holocaust Memorial Centre

5151 Cote Ste. Catherine Road

Montreal, Quebec
Canada H3W 1M6
phone: (514) 345-2605
fax: (514) 344-2651
e-mail: mhmc@accent.net

Holocaust Education and Memorial Centre of Toronto

4600 Bathurst Street
North York, Ontario
Canada M2R 3V2
phone: (416) 631-5689
fax: (416) 635-0925
e-mail: pzilbermanfeduja.org
Web: http//www.feduja.org

Vancouver Holocaust Centre Society

#50-950 West 41st Avenue
Vancouver, British Columbia
Canada V5Z 2N7
phone: (604) 264-0499
fax: (604) 264-0497
e-mail: holedctr@cybestore.ca

Germany

House of the Wannsee Conference

Am GroBen Wannsee 56-58
14109 Berlin
Germany
phone: 030/80-50-00-10
fax: 030/80-50-01-27

Stiftung Topography des Terrors

Budapester Strasse 40
D-10787 Berlin
Germany
phone: 49-30-25 45 090
fax: 49-30 2613002

Great Britain (United Kingdom)

Beth Shalom Holocaust Memorial & Education Centre

Laxton, Newark
Nottinghamshire
NG22 0PA England
phone: (+44) 1623-836627
fax: (+44) 1623-836647

Israel

Yad Vashem

P.O.B. 3477
Jerusalem
91304 Israel
phone: 972-2-6751611
fax: 972-2-6433511
e-mail: edu@yad-vashem.org.il
Web: www.yad-vashem.org.il

Beit Theresienstadt

Kibbutz Givat hayim-ihud
Mobile Post Emek Hefer
38935 Israel

phone: 972-6-6369515
fax: 972-6-6369611
e-mail: atresi@study.haifa.ac.il
Web: www.cet.ac.il/terezin

Beit Lohamei Haghetaot

Kibbutz Lohamei-Haghetaot
D.N. Western Galilee
25220 Israel
phone: 972-4-995-8080
fax: 972-4-995-8007

Japan

Holocaust Education Center/Hiroshima Japan

866 Nakatsuhara
Miyuki Fukuyama-City
Hiroshima Pref.
Japan 720
phone: (81) 849-55-0552
fax: (81) 849-55-8001
e-mail: hecjpn@urban.or.Jp

Russia

Russian Holocaust Research and Educational Center

Bulatnikovsky pas. 14-4-77
Moscow 113403
Russia
phone: (095) 383-6242
fax: (095) 383-6242
e-mail: altman@glas.apc.org

Ukraine

Kharkov Holocaust Center

P.O.B. 4756
Kharkov 310002
Ukraine
phone: 0572-436887

United States

California

Martyrs Memorial and Museum of the Holocaust of the Jewish Federation Council
6505 Wilshire Boulevard
Los Angeles, CA 90048
phone: (213) 852-3242
fax: (213) 951-0349

Simon Wiesenthal Center/ Museum of Tolerance
9760 West Pico Boulevard
Los Angeles, CA 90035-4792
phone: (310) 553-9036
fax: (310) 227-5558
library fax: (310) 277-6568
e-mail: library@wiesenthal.com
Web: http://www.wiesenthal.com

The Holocaust Center of Northern California
639 14th Avenue
San Francisco, CA 94118
phone: (415) 751-6040,
(415) 751-6041
fax: (415) 751-6735
e-mail: Bgoodman@juno.com

Colorado

Holocaust Awareness Institute
University of Denver
2199 South University Boulevard
Denver, CO 80208
phone: (303) 871-3013
fax: (303) 871-3137
e-mail: dmichael@dn.edu

Connecticut

Fortunoff Video Archive for Holocaust Testimonies
P.O. Box 802840

Sterling Memorial Library
Yale University
New Haven, CT 06520-8240
phone: (203) 432-1879
e-mail: loren.burns@yale.edu
Web: http://www.library.yale.edu/
testimonies/homepage.html

Delaware

Halina Wind Preston Holocaust Education Center
P.O. Box 2193
Wilmington, DE 19899
phone: (302) 427-2100
fax: (302) 427-2438

Florida

Holocaust Outreach Center
Florida Atlantic University
College of Education
777 Glades Road
P.O. Box 3091
Boca Raton, FL 33431
phone: (561) 367-2929
fax: (561) 367-3613
e-mail: EHECKLER@ACC.SAU.EDU

Mania Nudel Holocaust Learning Center
David Posnack Jewish Center
5850 South Pine Island Road
Davie, FL 33328
phone: (954) 434-4999, ext. 314
fax: (954) 434-1741

Tampa Bay Holocaust Memorial Museum and Education Center
5001-113th Street
Madeira Beach, FL 33708
phone: (813) 392-4678
fax: (813) 393-0236
e-mail: 102477.1162@compuserv.com

Web: http:\\zipmall.com\holo-caust.htm

Holocaust Memorial Resource & Education Center of Central Florida
851 North Maitland Avenue
Maitland, FL 332751
phone: (407) 628-0555
fax: (407) 628-1079

Holocaust Documentation and Education Center, Inc.
Florida International University
North Miami Campus
3000 NE 145 Street
North Miami, FL 33181
phone: (305) 919-5690
fax: (305) 919-5691
e-mail: xholocau@servak.fiu.edu

Georgia
The Lillian and A. J. Weinberg Center for Holocaust Education of the William Berman Jewish Heritage Museum
The Spring Center
1440 Spring Street NE
Atlanta, GA 30309-2837
phone: (404) 873-1661
fax: (404) 874-7043

Illinois
Zell Holocaust Memorial/Zell Center for Holocaust Studies of Spertus Institute of Jewish Studies
618 South Michigan Avenue
Chicago, IL 60605
phone: (312) 922-9012
fax: (312) 922-6406

Holocaust Memorial Foundation of Illinois
4255 West Main Street
Skokie, IL 60076-2063
phone: (847) 677-4640
fax: (847) 677-4684
e-mail: 7557.1427@compuserve.com

Kansas
Midwest Center for Holocaust Education
5801 West 115 Street, Suite 106
Shawnee Mission, KS 62211-1800
phone: (913) 327-8190
fax: (913) 327-8193
e-mail: SHOAHED@A.CRL.COM

Maine
Holocaust Human Rights Center of Maine
Box 4645
Augusta, ME 04330-1664
phone: (207) 993-2620
fax: (207) 993-2620
e-mail: nicholssk@juno.com

Massachusetts
Hatikvah Holocaust Education & Resource Center
1160 Dickinson Street
Springfield, MA 01108
phone: (413) 737-4313
fax: (413) 737-4348

Michigan
Holocaust Memorial Center
6602 West Maple Road
West Bloomfield, MI 48322-3005
phone: (810) 661-0840
fax: (810) 661-4204
e-mail: info@holocaustcenter.org
Web: http://holocaustcenter.org

Minnesota
Holocaust Resource Center
8200 W. 33rd Street
Minneapolis, MN 55426
phone: (612) 935-0316

Center for Holocaust Education
St. Cloud State University Stewart
Hall 125
St. Cloud, MN 56301
phone: (320) 255-3293
fax: (320) 654-5337

Missouri
**Holocaust Museum and Learning
Center/St. Louis**
12 Millstone Campus Drive
St. Louis, MO 63146
phone: (314) 432-0020
fax: (314) 432-1277

New Hampshire
**Holocaust Resource Center—
Keene State College**
Mason Library
Keene State College
Box 3201, 229 Main Street
Keene, NH 03435-3201
phone: (603) 358-2490
fax: (603) 358-2745
e-mail: childebr@keene.edu

New Jersey
**The Holocaust Museum and
Education Center of the
Deleware Valley**
2393 West Marlton Pike
Cherry Hill, NJ 08002
phone: (609) 665-6100
fax: (609) 665-0074

**Holocaust Resource Center of
the Jewish Federation of
Clifton-Pasaic**
199 Scoles Avenue
Clifton, NJ 07012
phone: (201) 777-7031
fax: (201) 777-6701

**The Julius and Dorothy
Koppleman Holocaust/Genocide
Resource Center**
Rider University
2083 Lawrenceville Road
Lawrenceville, NJ 08648
phone: (609) 896-5345
fax: (609) 895-5684
Web: holctr@rider.edu

**Center for Holocaust Studies—
Brookdale Community College**
765 Newman Springs Road
Lincroft, NJ 07738
phone: (908) 224-2769

**Drew University Center for
Holocaust Studies**
Rose Memorial Library/301
Madison, NJ 07940
phone: (201) 408-3600
fax: (201) 408-4768

**Center for Holocaust and
Genocide Studies—Ramapo
College**
Ramapo College Library
505 Ramapo Valley Road
Mahwah, NJ 07430
phone: (201) 529-7409
fax: (201) 529-6654

College of St. Elizabeth/Holocaust Education Resource Center
2 Convent Road
Morristown, NJ 07960
phone: (973) 290-4351
fax: (973) 290-4389
e-mail: sepinwal@liza.st-elizabeth.edu

Holocaust Resource Center— The Richard Stockton College of New Jersey
Pomona, NJ 08240
phone: (609) 652-4699
fax: (609) 748-5543

Holocaust Resource Center of Kean College
Thompson Library
Second Floor
Kean College
Union, NJ 07083
phone: (908) 527-3049

New York
Holocaust Resource Center and Archives
Queensborough Community College
22-05 56th Avenue
Bayside, NY 11364
phone: (718) 225-1617
fax: (718) 631-6306
e-mail: hrcaho@dorsai.org

The Manhattan College Resource Center
Manhattan College
Manhattan College Parkway
Bronx, NY 10471
phone: (718) 862-7248
fax: (718) 862-8044

Holocaust Resource Center of Buffalo
1050 Maryvale Drive
Cheektowaga, NY 14225
phone: (716) 634-9535
fax: (716) 634-9625

Holocaust Memorial and Education Center of Nassau County
Welwyn Preserve
100 Crescent Beach Road
Glen Cove, NY 11542
phone: (516) 571-8040
fax: (516) 571-8041

Holocaust Survivors and Friends in Pursuit of Justice
800 New Loudon Road
Suite 400
Latham, NY 12110
phone: (518) 785-0035
fax: (518) 783-1557

ADL Braun Holocaust Institute
823 United Nations Plaza
New York, NY 10017
phone: (212) 885-7804
fax: (212) 867-0779
e-mail: adlbraun@mindspring.com
Web: wwwadl.org

Anne Frank Center USA, Inc.
584 Broadway, Suite 408
New York, NY 10012
phone: (212) 431-7993
fax: (212) 431-8375
e-mail: Afexhibit@aol.com
Web: www.annefrank.com

A Living Memorial to the Holocaust—Museum of Jewish Heritage
First Place at Battery Park
New York, NY 10280

Westchester Holocaust Commission
Manhattanville College
2900 Purchase Street
Purchase, NY 10577
phone: (914) 696-0738
fax: (914) 696-0843
e-mail: WestHoloCommMSN.COM

Center for Holocaust Awareness and Information (CHAI)
Jewish Community Federation of Greater Rochester
441 East Avenue
Rochester, NY 14607
phone: (716) 461-0290
fax: (716) 461-0912
e-mail: JESD@eznet.net (Subject: Attn: Barbara)

North Dakota
The Holocaust Resource Center
c/o The West Rivers Teacher's Center
1679 6th Avenue West
Dickinson, ND 58601
phone: (701) 227-2139
e-mail: pgant@eagle.dsu.nodak.edu

Ohio
Dayton Holocaust Resource Center
100 East Woodbury Drive
Dayton, OH 45415
phone: (513) 278-7444
fax: (513) 832-2121

Holocaust Resource Center of Toledo
6465 Sylvania Avenue
Sylvania, OH 43560
phone: (519) 885-4485
fax: (519) 885-3207

Oregon
Oregon Holocaust Resource Center
2043 College Way
Warner 2S
Forest Grove, OR 97116
phone: (503) 244-6284
fax: (503) 246-7553
e-mail: boasj1@pacificu.edu

Pennsylvania
Allentown Jewish Archives/Holocaust Resource Center
702 North 22nd Street
Allentown, PA 18104
phone: (215) 821-5500
fax: (215) 821-8946

The National Catholic Center for Holocaust Education
Seton Hill College
Greensburg, PA 15601
phone: (412) 830-1033
fax: (412) 830-4611
e-mail: ncche@setonhil.edu

Holocaust Oral History Archive of Gratz College
Old York Road & Melrose Avenue
Melrose Park, PA 19027
phone: (215) 635-7300, ext. 30
fax: (215) 635-7320

Holocaust Center of the UJF of Greater Pittsburgh
242 McKee Place
Pittsburgh, PA 15213
phone: (412) 682-7111
fax: (412) 622-2223
e-mail: ujf.pgh.lhurwitz@ globalaccess.net

**Holocaust Museum and Resource
Center of the Scranton–
Lackawanna Jewish Federation**
601 Jefferson Avenue
Scranton, PA 18510
phone: (717) 961-2300, ext. 37

Rhode Island
**Rhode Island Holocaust
Memorial Museum and
Educational Outreach Center**
4041 Elmgrove Avenue
Providence, RI 09206
phone: (401) 453-7860
fax: (401) 861-8806

Texas
**The Dallas Memorial Center
for Holocaust Studies**
7900 Northaven Road
Dallas, TX 75230
phone: (214) 750-4654
fax: (214) 750-4672

**El Paso Holocaust Museum
and Study Center**
401 Wallenberg Drive
El Paso, TX 79912
phone: (915) 833-5656
fax: (915) 584-0243
Web: http://www.huntel.com

Holocaust Museum Houston
5401 Caroline Street
Houston, TX 77004
phone: (713) 942-8000
fax: (713) 942-7953
Web: http://www.hmh.org

Washington State
**Washington State Holocaust
Education Resource Center**
2031 Third Avenue
Seattle, WA 98121
phone: (206) 441-5747
fax: (206) 443-0303

Washington, D.C.
**United States Holocaust
Memorial Museum**
100 Raoul Wallenberg Place, SW
(15th Street & Independence
 Avenue)
Washington, D.C. 20024-2150
phone: (202) 488-0400
fax: (202) 488-2690
e-mail: education@ushmm.org
          research@ushmm.org
          library@ushmm.org
          archive@ushmm.org
Web: http://www.ushmm.org

Author Index

Subject Index

Photo Credits

Page 7: Estelle Bechoefer, courtesy of USHMM Photo Archives; page 11: Aron Raboy, courtesy of USHMM Photo Archives; pages 20, 51: National Archives; page 26: Janina Zimnowodzki, courtesy of USHMM Photo Archives; page 31: Benjamin Ferencz, courtesy of USHMM Photo Archives; pages 34, 37: courtesy of USHMM Photo Archives; page 38: Prof. Leopold Pfefferberg-Page, courtesy of USHMM Photo Archives; page 39: Stadtarchiv Munchen, courtesy of USHMM Photo Archives; page 41: Archive of Mechanical Doc.—Warsaw, courtesy of USHMM Photo Archives; page 44: Berta Hertz, courtesy of USHMM Photo Archives; page 68: YIVO Instutute for Jewish Research, courtesy of USHMM Photo Archives.

Maps and graphs ©Blackbirch Press, Inc.